It's Great to Be a Guy!

JARROD SECHLER
with **Dannah Gresh**

HARVEST HOUSE PUBLISHERS
EUGENE, OREGON

Cover and interior design by DesignByJulia.com, Colorado
Cover illustration by Julia Ryan / DesignByJulia.com
Interior spot illustrations and doodles: Julia Ryan and Shutterstock.com
Interior images (numbers indicate page location): © Shutterstock: 3, 84, 93, 95: donatas 1205; 14, 56, 100: SergiyN; 16: Tom Wang; 23 : Jaimie Duplass; 27: Glenda; 34: Werner Heiber; 38: Funny Solution Studio; 40: Blaj Gabriel; 45, 121: J.M. Gelpi; 49: Crystal Kirk; 51: Samuel Borges Photography; 52: ml; 58: wavebreakmedia; 64,99: Tracy Whiteside; 67: Monkey Business Images; 69, 70, 74, 76, 78, 81: Celig; 73, 97: auremar; 75: Basheera Designs; 85: stockyimages; 86: Donna Ellen Coleman; 113: Michael Jung; 115: Rob Marmion; 117: Kalmatsuy; 119: Catalin Petolea
Photo of Jarrod on page 5 by Sam Zubler

IT'S GREAT TO BE A GUY!

Copyright © 2016 Dannah Gresh
Published by Harvest House Publishers
Eugene, Oregon 97408
www.harvesthousepublishers.com

ISBN 978-0-7369-6278-0 (pbk.)
ISBN 978-0-7369-6279-7 (eBook)

Library of Congress Cataloging-in-Publication Data

Names: Sechler, Jarrod, author.
Title: It's great to be a guy! / Jarrod Sechler with Dannah Gresh.
Description: Eugene, Oregon : Harvest House, 2016.
Identifiers: LCCN 2015040912 | ISBN 9780736962780 (pbk.)
Subjects: LCSH: Boys—Religious life—Juvenile literature. | Boys—Conduct of
  life—Juvenile literature. | Boys—Psychology—Juvenile literature. |
  Puberty—Juvenile literature. | Teenage boys—Physiology—Juvenile
  literature.
Classification: LCC BV4541.3 .S43 2016 | DDC 248.8/2--dc23 LC record available at http://
lccn.loc.gov/2015040912

Contents

From the second you were born, your body has been in transition to become a man. It all seems to be so barely noticeable, but pretty soon puberty strikes and you wonder what on earth is happening to you.

The word "awkward" comes to mind. But don't worry. Tens of millions of guys are going through the same things you're about to go through:

- Your body may be thickening.

- You're growing taller by the second.

- At some point your voice might squeak like a mouse— and you can be sure it'll happen at the most embarrassing moment possible.

- The hair on your head may be getting thicker and more oily.

- And hair is appearing in the most surprising places.

- One thing is for sure: you'll stink!

[Welcome to puberty!]

These next few years are going to be an incredible adventure for you. I want you to know I'm honored to be your guide as you work through this book. I've based these pages on God's Word and, since 2 Timothy 3:16 says that all Scripture is inspired by God and is useful for teaching us the correct way to live, I'm 100 percent positive I'm using the right source.

Look at this book as if it was an instruction manual attached to your ankle when you were born. It gives instructions on how you operate, how you're powered, and what to do if you're not working like you should.

Years ago, when I was where you are now, a lot of good happened—as well as some bad stuff. Looking back, it would have been great to have this book then, since I was so unprepared. Through these pages, you'll be able to see the future—to know what's coming and to anticipate it rather than to be constantly surprised and confused by the crazy changes in your body and mind.

I hope you'll begin to understand that God designed your body and mind to be most fulfilled as you glorify and enjoy Him. He has a perfect plan for your exact design even if you can't understand it all yet.

You'll quickly see that the Bible has a *lot* to say about your body and its purpose, and that's the main reason I'm writing this to you. After looking at Scripture and God's plan, you're going to know without a doubt that **it's great to be a guy!**

I'm also going to get practical. Because you don't have to go through life smelling like your armpits. There's this thing called deodorant. (More on that in chapter 3.) And there'll be answers to questions about what's going on below the belt in chapter 7.

It's time to discover what the Bible tells us about taking care of this amazing vessel He has created…your body!

[You've got this, dude!]

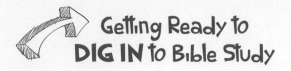

Getting Ready to
DIG IN to Bible Study

In this book I'm going to remind you to use one of the most powerful organs you have. It's not a muscle, but scientists say it's like a muscle in that it gets stronger with use. What organ do you think we're talking about?

The brain!

FOUR THINGS YOU MIGHT NOT KNOW ABOUT YOUR BRAIN (BUT SHOULD!)

1 Your brain is made up of about 75 percent water.
No wonder it's so important to drink plenty of water during the day. Make sure to keep your brain hydrated by drinking 1.5-2 liters of water every single day (that's about the size of a big soda bottle…and *no*, soda doesn't count).

2 Your brain thinks at a speed of 150-200 miles per hour.
That's about the same speed as a NASCAR race car! To keep your thinking speed up, make sure to eat healthy food and get plenty of exercise.

3 Your brain won't let you tickle yourself.
Your brother or sister may think it's funny to tickle you, but your brain doesn't; it actually thinks your body is under attack! Your brain knows if you're getting a real tickle-attack from your dad, or if you are trying to trick it. Go ahead and try it.

4 Your brain never sleeps, even when you do.
Your brain actually continues to think even after you fall asleep—this is why you dream. Humans typically can't remember most of our dreams when we wake up, but your brain is still trying to figure out why you almost tripped in the hallway long after your snooze.

The skill I'll teach you to muscle up your brain with God's Word is *meditation*. So, before you get into the great subject of your body, I'd like to take a little time to introduce you to meditation. This practice session even offers meditation verses to get you kick-started on this biblical journey through puberty.

What Is Meditation?

Well, you might think it's some crazy, weird thing only girls do while sitting cross-legged in a yoga position and humming. That's not true at all. That kind of meditation is just a sad fake for God's original. Let's see if I can help you get an idea of what God thinks meditation should look like.

To begin with, some Christians are so rigid about praying all the time, they never study. And some Christians are so consumed study- ing, studying, studying the Bible that they don't take time to pray.

Some Christians are really rigid about studying, studying, studying the Bible!

STUDIER

Some Christians are so consumed with praying all the time, they never study!

PRAY-ER

The risk for the **studier** is that his faith gets stuck in his head. He never has the *heart* to follow God because he's always arguing or defending what he *thinks* about God.

The risk for the **pray-er** is that his faith is all about his heart. He makes decisions to follow God based on how he *feels* and forgets to think about what God has already told him in His written Word. (God will never ask you to do something that disagrees with the Bible.)

MEDITATOR

But then there's a third type of person. A **meditator** studies the Bible and then asks God to help him understand it while he prays. A wise pastor once said that meditation is what happens when studying and praying crash into each other!

I'm going to keep this simple. Most of the Bible verses you'll need are printed right in this book. The only thing you'll need are some different colored highlighters, markers, or pencils

These are your meditation tools. Got 'em? Okay. Let's just get them warmed up by practicing meditation.

DIG IN by Studying Psalm 139:13-16

Throughout this book, you'll see this symbol inviting you to "dig in." This means you're about to *study* God's Word, kind of like an archaeologist studies the ground to uncover mysteries, secrets, and stories. So plop on your hard hat and get ready to dig. Let's give it a try, okay?

Let's do a little digging to see if God really does want us to practice meditation. After all, you shouldn't take our word for it.

Psalm 139 talks a lot about your body. It's written by the man of all men: King David. (A good guy to learn from when it comes to being a guy, don't you think?) He's writing about his body, but we know these things are true about *our* bodies too.

In these lines below from Psalm 139, **circle the words "you" or "your" with a blue marker every time it shows up.**

✏️ Psalm 139:13-16

For you formed my inward parts;

you knitted me together in my mother's womb.

I praise you, for I am fearfully and wonderfully made.

Wonderful are your works;

my soul knows it very well.

My frame was not hidden from you,

when I was being made in secret,

intricately woven in the depths of the earth.

Your eyes saw my unformed substance;

in your book were written, every one of them,

the days that were formed for me,

when as yet there was none of them.

David writes these Bible verses almost as if he's writing a personal letter to someone he refers to as "you." In Psalm 139, who do you think the words "you" and "your" refer to? **Write your answer in the space below:**

The answer is God. God created David (and you and me), and in this passage we read a lot of words that describe *how* He created us. What kinds of verbs or action words describe how God made David? Grab a red highlighter or marker. **In that passage from Psalm 139, circle any of these action words in red.**

Now, fill in the blanks below by writing what God did to create you.

1. _____   **2.** _____

     3. _____

For puzzle answers go to page 123.

Are those three things *accidental* or *intentional*? **Circle your choice with your favorite color.** (My favorite color is red.)

Based on what you're reading, **circle the sentence below that God would have been most likely to say when you were born:**

"WHOOPS! I MADE A GUY?"

OR   "THERE HE IS! THE WORK OF ART I PLANNED ALL ALONG."

I vote strongly that he said, *"There he is! The work of art I planned all along."* How do we know this? Because no one ever weaves, knits, or forms something without carefully laying out a plan. All of these actions require planning. Weaving and knitting even require math! God *planned* you. *Formed* your body. *Wove* you together. And *knit* you into a masterpiece.

Puzzle Craze

The Uses of Your Body

Your body might seem to be made for clothes or exercise or eating, but God's purposes for it are so much more important. **Look up each of the Bible verses below and discover what your body is in God's eyes.**

CLUES

Each word speaks of something that your body is for God.
(*Big hint: Like the word "vessel."*)

ACROSS
3. 1 Corinthians 3:16-17

DOWN
1. 1 Peter 2:5
2. Ephesians 2:19-22

For puzzle answers go to page 123.

LOOK Inside yourself

After you "dig in" by becoming a studier of the Bible, it's time to get ready to become a **pray-er**. It takes me a long time to sit in God's presence and really sense Him. I like to sit with my hands open until I am aware that He is there. It takes some time. This is kind of the bridge between studying and praying. When you see the "Look Inside" symbol, it means I'm getting ready to ask you some super-personal questions. Ready?

1 Select one from each set by putting a check mark by each thing you believe about your body. I am (or I feel as if I am)...

_____ Wonderfully made   _____ Imperfectly crafted

_____ Seen and known by God _____ Alone and afraid

_____ A house fit for God   _____ Unworthy of being God's home

2 Fill in the blank, selecting one of the areas above where you hope God can change you.

I wish I were more _____.

3 Based on what you learned today in our practice meditation about your body, do you believe what God says about your body? **Circle one of these answers.**

- I think I believe what God says about my body.
- I seem more influenced by what the world says about my body than what God says.
- I'm a little confused and need to keep studying and praying.

4 What do you think you need to do based on what you've just studied while "digging in"?

Reach UP and Talk to GOD

When you see this graphic,

you're going to add praying to your studying. Some guys like to write their prayers down in a journal. To help you learn how to do that, I'm going to help you write your prayers to God based on what you've just studied. **First, fill in the blanks to personalize your prayer and then pray your prayer out loud.**

Dear _____ **(your favorite name for God),** You are so___ _____ **(your favorite descriptive word for God)!** I praise You for who You are and for creating me and my body. I want to believe what You say about my body and it's worth. Please help me, especially in the area of _____. I am really struggling in this area and this makes me feel _____.

Will You help me? As I start this Bible study, I promise to meditate by studying the Bible and then praying. I look forward to what You'll do in me to change me. I'm feeling very: ____ excited ____ overwhelmed.

I give this emotion to You. In Jesus' name,

_____

(sign here)

Congratulations! You just meditated. Now that you've practiced, we're ready to meditate on God's truth about your body. Welcome to **It's Great to Be a Guy!**

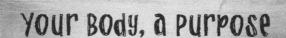

Your Body, a Purpose

You were bought with a price. So glorify God in your body.
1 CORINTHIANS 6:20

I started puberty later than the other boys in my class. They began to grow muscles, mustaches, and armpit hair, and to develop into men while I remained a boy. When we were required to change clothes for gym class in the seventh-grade boys' locker room, it became readily evident to everyone who were the men and who were the boys. I was a boy. I longed to be a man. It didn't really help that my dad was a manly man. He'd played defensive tackle in college and was feared by men and boys alike. He was a teacher in the school I attended, and he commanded the respect of everyone by his stature alone. I, on the other hand, was known by some of my extended family members as "Little Jer" because of my meager frame.

It was not a nickname I liked. I had a cousin my age who would dominate me in wrestling, boxing, foot races, and anything else physical we set out to do.

Yep, I was a boy who longed to be a man.

In about eighth grade the upperclassmen on the football team at my school presented me with a new nickname. Because I'd begun to grow taller yet still lagged behind my classmates in physical development, I became known around school as "Noodle." I was tall, skinny, and awkward. All hopes of manhood seemed lost. I was convinced I'd never be the man my father was or the man my cousin was becoming. Nor would I ever be able to compete with other males my age. I began to think that I might always be just a boy who longed to be a man.

It wasn't until about ninth and tenth grades that I began to really grow into my manly body. Since then I've outgrown almost every male from my middle school days. Today I stand six feet two and weigh 225 pounds. No one has called me "Noodle" (or any other floppy wet pasta names) in decades. And, oh, about that cousin who dominated me in everything—I think he stopped growing in about ninth grade. The last time I saw him, he commented that I was definitely not "Little Jer" anymore.

BODY HOMEWORK

Instead of telling you everything about growing up, I'm going to give you just a few key ideas in this book. It's a broad overview of the changes ahead, not a play-by-play game plan.

To help you understand these, at times you're gonna need to talk with a guy who's already all man— your dad or granddad, or a big brother, uncle, or trustworthy neighbor. There's no better time to start that conversation than now. So here's today's homework: pick the growing-up topic that most terrifies you—wet dreams, deodorant, shaving, jock straps, or whatever— and go ask a reliable older guy about it. Trust us; he'll be honored when you ask.

If I could give you one piece of advice for learning about your body it would be this: don't wait. Talk with someone now. Talk early and talk often.

What do I mean by "talk often"? I mean that this is not a taboo topic of conversation. None of the topics in this book are off-limits. In fact, they're just everyday conversation once you get comfortable with them. Every guy wakes up having had a wet dream. Every guy needs deodorant so his armpits don't create a stench that'd kill Bigfoot (or at least your mother). Every guy wonders when he's ready to shave. And every guy has to figure out how to use a jockstrap. And we're gonna talk about it all. These are common and ordinary things we all go through.

every guy has to figure it out

You have two choices when it comes to puberty: suffer through it alone, or literally MAN UP and do what it takes to get with the plan. **Which one do you choose?**

THREE FACTS ABOUT PUBERTY EVERY GUY MUST KNOW

FACT #1: Every guy's body is different and every guy develops at a different rate.

On average, a guy will start puberty around his tenth or eleventh birthday. Some guys get started earlier, and others might be twelve or thirteen before they notice any changes.

What kind of changes? Here are a few of them, and the stages during which they're likely to occur. (More on many of these big events later in the book!)

Pubescent Timeline

1 STAGE ONE: You may notice hairs growing around the base of the penis (they're called "pubic hair"), your testicles will slowly get larger, and the scrotum (the loose skin around your testicles) will get darker and looser.

2 STAGE TWO: Your voice may begin to deepen, probably beginning with some cracks and squeaks. Your body will thicken as you gain pounds, and you'll go through a crazy growth spurt as you get taller. Your penis gets longer and darker, and pubic hairs get crazy curly and start to grow all over everything down there.

3 STAGE THREE: Everything in stage two keeps happening, plus you'll start to get facial hair. And the hair on your body—well, let's just say it takes on a life of its own. Your pubic hair may extend up the belly. You're physically a man. *Congratulations.* (But there is no certificate.)

FACT #2: All the changes in your body are happening for a reason.

God has arranged all that's necessary to make your body fully ready for your becoming a father one day. (It's that simple. You don't have to do anything to make puberty happen).

FACT #3: These changes are normal and safe, though they may seem awkward or uncomfortable.

It's been said that no one likes change except a baby in a wet diaper. Change is scary because we have no idea what it will bring. If you feel a little nervous about your body changing, don't worry. I survived it and I'm here to tell you that you will too.

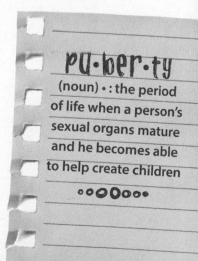

pu·ber·ty

(noun) • : the period of life when a person's sexual organs mature and he becomes able to help create children

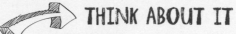

THINK ABOUT IT

**Use this box to create a list of questions
you do NOT want to forget to ask!**

Meditation 1

Your Body, a Purpose

o guts. No glory." It's true—from the time of the gladiators until now, being a man takes courage—and so does bringing glory to God. Puberty can be confusing, annoying, and somewhat discouraging, but knowing what to expect will give you the confidence that God knows what He's doing.

Remember, having confidence in God is what produces true courage in the first place. You'll see how that worked in David's life in the next section.

> [**FACT: God has a much bigger purpose in mind for your body . . . and I'm going to show you how cool that is.**]

DIG IN by Studying 1 Samuel 17:32-37, 41-50

You probably know the Old Testament story of David the shepherd boy who took on a giant named Goliath. The famous Renaissance artist Michelangelo, in his famous solid-marble sculpture of David, depicts him as an extremely muscular dude. The reality, however, is that David was probably more of a gangly teenager than a seasoned warrior. David simply believed he'd been created to glorify God with the body he'd been given, regardless of his physical stature. **Let's take a look at the story, beginning when David announces he will take on the titan:**

32 "Don't worry about this Philistine," David told Saul. "I'll go fight him!" **33** "Don't be ridiculous!" Saul replied. "There's no way you can fight this Philistine and possibly win! You're only a boy, and he's been a man of war since his youth." **34** But David persisted. "I have been taking care of my father's sheep and goats," he said. "When a

lion or a bear comes to steal a lamb from the flock, **35** I go after it with a club and rescue the lamb from its mouth. If the animal turns on me, I catch it by the jaw and club it to death. **36** I have done this to both lions and bears, and I'll do it to this pagan Philistine, too, for he has defied the armies of the living God! **37** The LORD who rescued me from the claws of the lion and the bear will rescue me from this Philistine!" Saul finally consented. "All right, go ahead," he said. "And may the LORD be with you!"... **41** Goliath walked out toward David with his shield

Did you know that the point at the end of Goliath's spear weighed as much as a bowling ball? 15 pounds!

bearer ahead of him, **42** sneering in contempt at this ruddy-faced

boy. **43** "Am I a dog," he roared at David, "that you come at me with a

stick?" And he cursed David by the names of his gods. **44** "Come over

here, and I'll give your flesh to the birds and wild animals!" Goliath

yelled. **45** David replied to the Philistine, "You come to me with

sword, spear, and javelin, but I come to you in the name of the LORD of

Heaven's Armies—the God of the armies of Israel, whom you have

defied. **46** Today the LORD will conquer you, and I will kill you and

cut off your head. And then I will give the dead bodies of your men to

the birds and wild animals, and the whole world will know that there

is a God in Israel! **47** And everyone assembled here will know that

the LORD rescues his people, but not with sword and spear. This is the

LORD's battle, and he will give you to us!" **48** As Goliath moved closer

to attack, David quickly ran out to meet him. **49** Reaching

into his shepherd's bag and taking out a stone, he hurled it with his

sling and hit the Philistine in the forehead. The stone sank in, and

Goliath stumbled and fell face down on the ground. **50** So David

triumphed over the Philistine with only a sling and a stone,

for he had no sword (1 Samuel 17:32-37,41-50 NLT).

Puzzle Craze

What's the Purpose of My Body?

You might feel like the most exciting purpose of your body is to make fart noises and throw a ball really, really far, but God has greater purposes for your body! **Look up each of the Bible verses below to discover the real purpose of your body.**

CLUES: Each word speaks of a purpose that YOUR body has for God. **Find the word in each of these verses!** (We used NIV.)

ACROSS

1. 1 Timothy 4:8
3. Philippians 1:20
5. 1 Corinthians 6:19-20 (ESV)

DOWN

2. Ephesians 2:19-22
4. 1 Corinthians 15:44

For puzzle answers go to page 123.

What's our purpose? God created us to glorify Him. That's our number one job.

To glorify God means to make Him **visible** or **known**—sort of the way the moon makes the sun known. The moon has no light of its own, but it can be seen as it reflects the light of the sun. In this way the moon "glorifies" the sun. God is like the sun, and we're meant to be like the moon.

Circle the specific thing we are supposed to use when we glorify or make God known.

You were bought with a price. So glorify God in your body (I Corinthians 6:20).

Specifically what part of us is supposed to glorify Him?

Our_____.

For puzzle answers go to page 123.

Our bodies are created and exist to glorify God. Much as you might enjoy making body noises, these are not the purposes of our bodies. But those things sort of humble us and make us laugh at ourselves, don't they? That's okay. Every great doctor, theologian, prayer warrior, banker, teacher, soldier, and father who has ever lived spent the first nine months of his life in a warm, safe womb (and the next nine months spitting up and needing diaper changes!) People never have been and never will be the superstars in this story of life. God Himself has always been and will always be the famous one. It is our job to make His fame more and more known *with our bodies.*

burping is not the purpose of our bodies

LOOK Inside Yourself

As males, we often think of glory in terms of athletic achievements. I played four years of football in high school and was an average player who got the job done, but I was never a star on the field. My crowning achievement on the football field occurred during my senior year—and it never really happened. I call it *The Greatest Pass I Never Threw.*

We were playing our rival team, the Rams of Southern Garrett. I was number 17, playing quarterback. Our halfback was number 7. We called a play that involved a direct snap to the halfback, and he threw a 71-yard touchdown pass to one of our receivers. Everyone saw the 7 on his jersey and assumed it was my number 17. Everyone thought I threw that pass. I mean *everyone.* My teammates, my friends, even my parents thought I'd finally done something big on the field. I even got the credit the next day in the newspaper! The reality, though, was that I wasn't a star. I was just average old me. I didn't deserve the glory.

The good news is that this isn't the kind of glory we're talking about when we look at 1 Corinthians 10:31. God isn't looking for you to glorify Him in front of hundreds, thousands, or even millions with your athletic talents. You don't have to play in the NFL, NBA, or NHL to bring Him glory. You do it by living out your average, ordinary, everyday life in ways that honor Him.

Two actions we do with our bodies are specifically named in 1 Corinthians 10:31. Circle them.

 So, whether you eat or drink, or whatever you do, do all to the glory of God.

Eating and drinking with our bodies can glorify God. But so can "whatever." Shaving, watching football, doing math, making your bed, or singing songs can glorify God.

What kinds of things do you like to do with your body? Write a Top Ten List below of your favorite ten activities. (Keep in mind that *everything* you write down can be for His glory.)

1. _____

2. _____

3. _____

4. _____

5. _____

6. _____

7. _____

8. _____

9. _____

10. _____

Reach UP and Talk to GOD

Dear Jesus,

Wow. This is deep stuff. I can see that the purpose of my body is to _____ God. Help me to eat and drink to _____ You. Today I thought of the following things I can do with my body to bring glory to You. They include _____, _____, _____, and _____. Thank You for showing me my purpose in Your plan. Forgive me for the times I've tried to be the superstar. I know that my purpose on earth is to make You look like the hero, and not me. In everything that I do, help me to point people straight to You. You alone are the famous one!

I love You, Jesus!

_____
(sign here)

Your Body, Its Practice

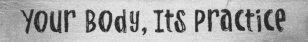

*So God created man in his own image, in the image of God
he created him; male and female he created them.*

GENESIS 1:27

YUP!

Sometimes we walk like them. Sometimes we talk like them. Sometimes we think or laugh like them. Almost all the time, we look like one of them. Yup, I'm always amazed at how many of the same characteristics we share with our parents. Some traits are part of our DNA before we're even born, but we also pick up a lot of these traits by spending time with our parents and observing how they do things. Some of the things we pick up are good, some maybe not so good.

Today we're going to take a look in the mirror and try to figure out who you look and act like. We're going to talk about how you might look like your mom or dad, but you also were created to look like God!

HERE WE GO!

Meditation 2

Your Body, Its Practice

We're going to start a bit backwards today, saving the Bible verses for later. Let's start by taking a good look at *you*.

LOOK Inside yourself

Determine whose image you bear. An image is a picture, statue, or a likeness of someone else. Whose image do you bear? That is, who do you look like? Your mom? Your dad? Your great grandma from Tokyo? Your uncle from Alaska?

Sometimes we figure this out best by taking it piece-by-piece. **Grab a mirror and look at each part of yourself carefully. When you've decided who you look like in a certain part of your body, write that person's name in the space provided. If you have trouble figuring one out, ask for help from someone who knows you and your family well.**

My **EYES** look like _____.

My **NOSE** looks like _____.

My **BODY TYPE** takes after _____.

The **SHAPE OF MY HEAD** matches _____.

I have _____'s **HAIR**.

And _____'s **HANDS**.

People say I **WALK** like _____.

And I **TALK** like _____.

That exercise wasn't easy if you've been adopted. In fact, it could make you sort of sad if you don't know what your biological mom and dad look like. I understand! My coauthor, Dannah Gresh, and her husband, Bob, have an adopted daughter named Autumn. Sometimes Bob and Dannah see themselves showing up in Autumn even though they didn't bring her into this world. For example, Dannah and Autumn both like to get things done early in the day. Autumn and Bob both laugh alike. Finding these commonalities is important if you don't look alike. Maybe you could try that. In fact, let's all try it, adopted or not.

Write a list of ways that you've become like your mom or dad in the space below. Maybe you both say the same phrase or sentence a lot. Maybe you both love ice cream or baseball. Pick as many of these things as you can think of.

BONUS!
LOOK
Inside
yourself

Chosen Image: Write down some ways you act like your mom or dad. Sometimes we're around people we live with and love so much that we become like them in the way we act.

DIG IN by Studying Genesis 1:26-31; 2 Corinthians 3:18

We turn again to another familiar story from the Bible—creation. No doubt you've heard the familiar phrase, "In the beginning, God created." This is where we find out just how God planned for us to *glorify* Him—to bring Him "glory." Remember that from chapter 1? **Write what the word "glorify" means by filling in the blanks below.** (If you need help, go back and review the meditation in the last chapter.)

To glorify God means to make Him

_____ or_____.

(Answers on page 123)

Today we're going to learn that God had this in mind all along—from the very point of creation. Way back then He was thinking of what you would look like. Yep, that fact has a lot to do with your image. **Use a bright yellow marker to circle the word "image" or any word that's like "image" (hint: "likeness") when you find it below.**

➥ **26** Then God said, "Let us make man in our image, after our

likeness. And let them have dominion over the fish of the sea and

over the birds of the heavens and over the livestock and over all the

earth and over every creeping thing that creeps on the earth."

27 So God created man in his own image, in the image of God he

created him; male and female he created them. **28** And God

blessed them. And God said to them, "Be fruitful and multiply and fill the earth and subdue it, and have dominion over the fish of the sea and over the birds of the heavens and over every living thing that moves on the earth." **29** And God said, "Behold, I have given you every plant yielding seed that is on the face of all the earth, and every tree with seed in Its fruit. You shall have them for food. **30** And to every beast of the earth and to every bird of the heavens and to everything that creeps on the earth, everything that has the breath of life, I have given every green plant for food." And it was so. **31** And God saw everything that he had made, and behold, it was very good. And there was evening and there was morning, the sixth day (Genesis 1:26-31).

According to the passage above, you weren't created in the image of your mother, or of your father, or of your grandparents, no matter whose nose you sport on the front of your face. You were created in the image of God, and He has an opinion about that. Let's see what it is. **Draw a bunch of big arrows pointing to the word in verse 31 that completes the sentence below. Then, fill in the blank:**

"And God saw everything that he had made,

and behold, it was very _____."

God makes it clear: the fact that you're made in His image is very **good!** This might be because we make God visible or known (we glorify Him) by looking like Him! How cool is that? And it gets even cooler!

Find two different colored markers; use them to circle the words "male" and "female" in Genesis 1:27 on page 30. Use different colors for each word. Now answer this question by filling in the two blanks:

> What two things does Genesis 1:27 specifically mention when it says that humans are created in the image of God?

1._____ **2.**_____

(Answers on page 123).

God specifically points out that our gender, or sex, is a trait that makes us look like Him. There are lots of things that make us god-like. Our brains. Our creativity. But God mentions only maleness and femaleness in Genesis when He says we're created in His image. It seems like being a guy is a BIG DEAL! (And so is being a girl!)

Any ideas on *why* He chose two very distinctly different genders to represent Him?

That's a super hard question, so we're going to help you. It's because God is three distinctly different persons, all in one being. He is God the Father, God the Son, God the Holy Spirit. He's three distinct persons and yet one being—the Trinity. The Hebrew word in the Bible for this unity is *echad.*

One male and one female are capable of being united by God into marriage. God created male and female to be distinctly different but capable of being united

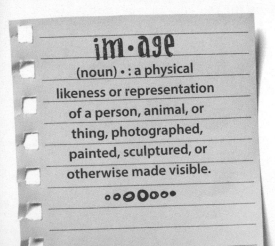

im·age

(noun) • : a physical likeness or representation of a person, animal, or thing, photographed, painted, sculptured, or otherwise made visible.

∘∘●◐∘∘•

into one. The Hebrew word in the Bible for this unity is also *echad*. Just look at this Bible verse:

That is why a man leaves his father and mother and is united to his wife, and they become one [echad] **flesh (Genesis 2:24 NIV).**

The male and the female are two distinct, independent humans but when they come together they are "echad." An ancient Jewish prayer cries out: "Hear, O Israel: The Lord our God, the Lord is one [*echad*]" (Deuteronomy 6:4).

If our purpose is to glorify God, our practice—the act that makes our purpose possible—is to embrace His image in us by being every bit the guy He created us to be.

What's our practice? God created us as males to reflect His image. That's how we glorify Him best.

This is super heavy-duty brain food, but I think you're capable of handling it all. Let's look at one more Bible verse while we're digging in. **Use your yellow marker again and circle the word "image."**

And we all, with unveiled face, beholding the glory of the Lord, are being transformed into the same image from one degree of glory to another. For this comes from the Lord who is the Spirit (2 Corinthians 3:18).

Using your yellow marker, underline the three-word verb in that verse that shows up just after the first mention of "the Lord."

You should have underlined "are being transformed." What does this say about the fact that we are made in God's image? **Write about it below.**

_____

_____

_____

_____

_____

_____

We are *still* being made to look more and more like Him. Through Christ you'll always be in the process of becoming the image of God. He transforms us continually into being what makes us most like Him and most capable of glorifying Him. He starts with the fact that you're a guy—then works on you from there!

YOU'RE A GUY!

Puzzle Craze

Find these important words in the word search below. As you do, remember what they mean and how they fit into your purpose to glorify God.

ECHAD   FEMALE   IMAGE   MALE   TRANSFORMED

F G D C W G B E V K N B S N D
D X E M Y Y L X R F W K B A B
Y K M M S A E Z T P T U P K Q
L A R J M E R H C S C B V O S
Y B O E Y R B Z I H C M D G N
R J F E Y A X L X D P B U H D
D B S J N E P X L Z Q S N Q M
D T N T V I J O Z E E S X P U
S V A O Y H M F H J J D D I D
A C R S D U P A X F Z C I A H
F E T H K L C B G Y M M K I U
F O V Q K T D J G E A T X W H
E C H A D C R N U L L K D Z I
T L Y U K L L X M L E F T N N
J K P M B P N V N Z G X G L I

For puzzle answers go to page 123.

LOOK
Inside
yourself

Embrace whose image you bear. This lesson is so important, let's take a second look inside your heart. This time I want to ask you this question: Can you accept and embrace the One whose image you bear?

Sometimes we don't really like certain things about us. Our hair maybe. Or we complain about our skin or other parts of our body. As guys, we don't often like how tall or short we are. In this way, we reject our mom's eyes, or our dad's hair, or our grandma's long crooked pointy finger. Is that rejection okay? I don't think it is. It's rejecting what God created. And in the passage you just studied, God says that what He created is **good!** You should believe that your nose, hair, eyes, and body are good.

Let's take this one step further. You're supposed to believe that being made in God's image is **good.** The fact that you're male and able to fulfill your purpose to glorify God as a guy is something you should embrace. Some people reject it, probably because they don't understand God's good purpose and plan or they're just confused.

[**You're a guy. That glorifies God. It's good!**]

It doesn't matter if you're a hunting, football loving, blue-wearing guy, or a painting, gymnastics-loving, yellow-wearing guy. God chose for you to be a guy.

 **THINK ABOUT IT**

What kind of guy are you? Will you choose to embrace being a guy no matter how unique you are?

REACH UP and TALK to GOD

Dear Jesus,

Here I am. A guy. Being a guy makes me feel _____. I did / didn't (**circle one**) know how important being a guy was, but now I have studied about it and realize more than ever that it's what helps other people to recognize You. It's how we glorify You. Here are some questions on my heart about being a guy (**write these out**):

1. _____

_____

2. _____

_____

3. _____

_____

I want to look like You so others can see You in me. Keep transforming me. I know that what You have created in me is **GOOD!**

In Jesus' name, amen!

YOUR BODY, GOD'S TEMPLE

Do you not know that you are God's temple and that God's Spirit dwells in you? If anyone destroys God's temple, God will destroy him. For God's temple is holy, and you are that temple.

1 CORINTHIANS 3:16-17

WOW!

I have a chocolate labradoodle named Willow. Her brother from the same litter, named Moose, belongs to Bob and Dannah Gresh (Dannah is my coauthor for this book). We like dogs, and would probably like yours too. **Take a moment to draw a picture of your dog on the next page, and include the dog's name and breed. If you don't have a dog, draw a picture of your cat (I love cats too), or anyone's pet you particularly like.**

Willow and Moose rest together after a long romp.

38

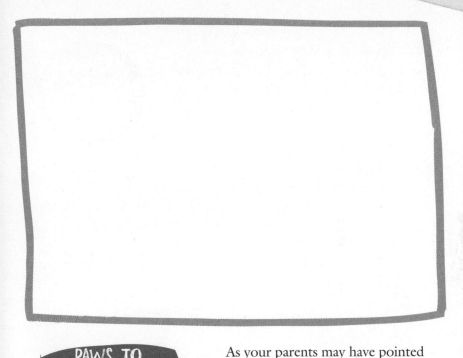

PAWS TO CONSIDER THE COST

Dogs need food, toys, beds, doctor visits, leashes, medicine, grooming, and occasional dog-sitting… so the average dog owner will spend between $1000 and $3000 per year on a dog. Over the course of a ten-year life span, that's $10,000 to $30,000 per dog!

As your parents may have pointed out to you, raising and caring for dogs costs money. A LOT of money! And when it's time to go away from home on a trip, you can't—until you find some other dog-crazy person who'll help you with your beloved four-footed critter. When we go away and ask people to take care of our dogs, it doesn't always go so well. Dannah's husband, Bob, can hardly stand the thought of Moose being alone. He's one of those dog-in-the-bed types. He's very picky about who gets to take care of Moose. The fact is, no one's likely to take care of our dogs the way we would.

Guess what? No one's going to take care of *you* quite the way you do either. And by now you've probably also realized that the human body, especially a body about to hit puberty, needs way more care than a puppy dog does.

am I ready to shave yet?

There are several places where the Bible tells us to take care of our bodies, and gives reasons as well. Today we'll look at what God says about your body and begin learning about important things like bathing, shaving, deodorant, and cleaning your face. Just as skills must be learned to cook a meal or play an instrument, you'll have things to learn in order to care for your body.

So let's go to school.

BODY BOOST 1: SOAP

Trust us, you're not always the best judge of what you smell like. Let's make sure the smells we're broadcasting to the world cooperate with our desire to have others near us. Commit yourself to daily or every-other-day baths or showers. Do this in the morning or at night, whenever it best fits your schedule. It's time to get serious about it.

BODY BOOST 2: FACE CARE

So what causes pimples, or acne? It's pretty complicated, because God's design of your body is crazy good. Your skin is full of pores (or hair follicles) that produce their own oils. The oil-producing glands in your pores are called sebaceous glands. Puberty hormones tell these sebaceous glands to increase production of skin oil, but sometimes the glands work a little overtime and dead skin cells or bacteria get trapped inside our pores along with too much oil. This produces a pimple.

Two things can help prevent pimples: keeping your face clean and keeping your hands clean. It helps when you wash your face regularly *before* the zits start to show up!

Once a pimple shows up, it's best to let it run its natural course. It'll most likely be gone within a week. If the pimple does turn white, that means the trapped oils and bacteria are near the surface and can be more safely "popped," though you should never deal with pimples unless your hands are washed and you're able to immediately put an antibacterial wash on the sore. If you can, resist the temptation to "pop" a pimple.

Best way to prevent pimples to begin with? **Wash your face every morning and night like clockwork,** but there's no need to wash more frequently or to scrub like crazy. Again, God's design is amazing. A simple wash will remove dead skin cells, which are the main culprit getting trapped in those open pores. If you use a moisturizing cream afterward, be sure it's "non-acnegenic," a fancy way to say it doesn't clog your pores. That tends to make acne worse.

BODY BOOST 3: DEODORANT

Time to start using deodorant every day. There are very few things as offensive to other people's noses as body odor. (I'm willing to bet your own nose has taught you that.)

Want to hear a simple rule that applies to much of life? *Less is more.* It can't get much easier than that, can it? Less deodorant. Less offending other people even with your good smells. It can be tempting to put on a lot of something that smells really good.

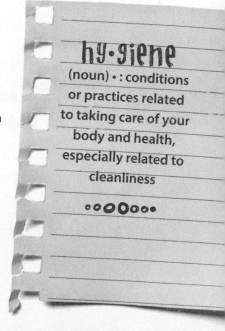

hy·giene

(noun) • : conditions or practices related to taking care of your body and health, especially related to cleanliness

BODY BOOST 4: RAZOR

Eventually you'll likely want to shave your emerging beard. Shaving's one of the more difficult hygiene practices to master. No one's good at it from the start—which is a bit of a scary thought, since a sharp object is the tool in question! There's no rush to begin, but once you do, you'll need to shave at least once a week.

BODY BOOST 5: WATER

Did you know that drinking water will make you healthier? It's true. Of course, it's also important for other reasons. Water helps you digest food, circulate blood, and even makes it easier to, um, "excrete." But drinking water will also help you have healthier looking skin. After all, your skin is an organ made up of cells, and cells are made of water. They need water to function well. If you don't drink enough water, your skin could become dry and itchy. Your goal should be to drink about 64 ounces a day. Having a water bottle with ounces marked on it will help you keep track.

Meditation 3

Your Body, God's Temple

I've heard horror stories of young guys so concerned about their body and its appearance that they went to extremes. They'd buy fancy gadgets to help straighten their nose or use some "natural" remedy for acne that had horrible side effects.

The truth is, you don't need to take extreme measures to take care of your skin, your hair, your teeth, or any other part of your body. There aren't any shortcuts to being clean and healthy either. Do the little things each day to take care of yourself and you'll look great.

- ☐ Wake up at _____ a.m.
- ☐ Make your bed.
- ☐ Eat breakfast and rinse your dishes.
- ☐ Brush teeth for three minutes (and floss!)
- ☐ Shower (don't forget your hair, feet, and armpits).
- ☐ Put on deodorant and brush hair.
- ☐ Hang up towel and put dirty clothes in laundry basket.

- ☐ Get dressed.
- ☐ Read the Bible, meditate, and pray.
- ☐ Check backpack to make sure all homework and books are there.
- ☐ Pack lunch.
- ☐ Put shoes on.
- ☐ Report to Mom and Dad for further instruction.
- ☐ Be completely ready to leave for school at _____ a.m.

Puzzle Craze

Unscramble this popular saying using the words below. They're in the correct order. All you have to do is unscramble the words.

enelCasnils _____

si _____ netx _____ ot_____

osedgslin _____.

Write the sentence out below.

_____ _____

_____ _____ _____.

Answer to puzzle on page 123.

Do you think that's a Bible verse? It sounds like one, but it's not. The Bible never says being clean on the outside is being like God. But the misunderstanding is an honest one. Here's why.

Many of the first-century Jews who followed Jesus believed that people who became Christians should continue following a lot of Old Testament rituals that had once made a person "clean" in God's sight. However, new followers of Jesus were given tremendous freedom, because they learned that rituals could never cleanse people's hearts—only Jesus can do that! When we ask Christ to dwell inside us, He makes our hearts clean.

His death on the cross makes all this possible (more on this straight ahead). Embracing this truth is what makes us a Christian. If you've never asked Jesus to be the Lord of your life and cleanse your inside, turn to the end of this chapter and read "The ABCs of Becoming a Christian."

DIG IN by Studying 1 Corinthians 3:16-17; 10:24; 3 John 1:2

As we look at the entire Bible, it seems there are three reasons to be clean. Let's look at each of them by studying a few passages. We're going to let you fill in the blanks, so pay close attention!

 16 Do you not know that you are God's temple and that God's Spirit dwells in you? 17 If anyone destroys God's temple, God will destroy him. For God's temple is holy, and you are that temple (1 Corinthians 3:16-17).

In the opening line, the verse above says that

"you are _____ _____."

Use your red marker to circle what you are. Then circle every time the phrase shows up in those verses.

being God's temple is cool!

A temple is a place where God lives. If you've asked Christ to be Lord of your life, His Spirit lives inside you. **You are God's temple**. Obviously, you want to take care of God's house, don't you? The first reason to take care of your body is that it is *God's temple*. **Write that in the space below.**

REASON 1: _____

➤ **Let no one seek his own good, but the good of his neighbor (1 Corinthians 10:24).**

Using the verse above, fill in the blanks in this statement.

No one _____ seek their own _____,

but the good of _____.

Being clean on the outside, as much as we are able, is kind of important for being close to other people. So, the second reason we should stay clean is the comfort of other people. We're supposed to look like God so we can help other people meet Him (remember our last meditation?). By not smelling bad and by presenting ourselves well, we can make sure others are comfortable around us. *Comfort of others* is the second reason to keep clean. **Write that in the space below.**

REASON 2: _____

Beloved, I pray that all may go well with you and that you may be in good health, as it goes well with your soul (3 John 2).

In this verse, circle the words "good health."

God wants you to be healthy, and being clean promotes good health. Some Old Testament laws contain very practical advice about hygiene. God told the Israelites not to touch dead bodies, which can carry disease. He told them to make soap because being clean protects us from disease. God wants us to be well. He wants us to be useful.

The final reason we should practice good hygiene is to be *healthy to serve God.* **Write that in the space below.**

REASON 3: _____

LOOK Inside yourself

On the next page you'll find the meditator guy we used earlier in the book. One who studies and prays generally ends up making wise decisions. This should include the area of taking care of your body. Let's consider him the model of health. **On his left side, write a list of all the wise choices he makes to be clean and healthy. On the right side of him, write a list of all the things that help you reach your goal of being clean and healthy.**

USE SOAP

Meditator's Healthy, Clean Habits

My Healthy, Clean Habits

_____ _____
_____ _____
_____ _____
_____ _____
_____ _____
_____ _____
_____ _____
_____ _____
_____ _____
_____ _____

My Healthy Clean Habit Goals

No one's perfect. Remember, you don't have to go to extremes to change anything about you. However, if you'd like to set simple goals based on what you learned today, **in the space below write down three goals you can use to start taking better care of yourself.**

1. _____

2. _____

3. _____

REACH UP and TALK to GOD

Hi, Jesus!

I'm ready to talk a bit about getting clean! I realize that my body is Your temple or house, so I want to take care of it for You. I also want to be able to be around other people and work closely with them, and I know I have to be clean for that. I think / don't think **(circle one)** I'm very healthy. I do have these good habits:

_____

_____. But I could

totally stand to work on these things: _____

_____.

Can You please teach me how to do this right? Motivate me to stay clean and eat right. Sometimes I can be lazy about that. Help me accept advice from other people about my cleaning habits. I confess that sometimes I get grumpy when people correct me. And most of all, help me to want super-clean insides. I want to love You, follow You, serve You, and be like You. That's more about my heart than anything else, so help me make that the most important thing of all!

I really love You!

_____

(sign here)

THE ABCS OF BECOMING A CHRISTIAN

Lots of people say they're Christians, but many of them probably are not. What a sad thing to think that going to church, being good, or calling yourself a Christian would be your ticket to heaven, all the while never having actually chosen to follow Jesus Christ in obedience. Jesus Himself said He was the only way to heaven: "I am the way, the truth, and the life. No one comes to the Father except through me" (John 14:6). Becoming a Christian isn't difficult, but many people are confused or distracted by things and actions that do not make them a Christian any more than walking on all fours makes me a dog!

A **Admit you are a sinner.** A person starts by confessing that he has sinned. He must be sorry for his sin and willing to stop. Whether you've been fighting with your siblings, cheating on tests, or bullying other kids, sin separates us from God. He is so perfect and holy, He cannot be in the presence of our unclensed sin. Romans 3:23 says, "All have sinned and fall short of the glory of God." There's that word "glory" again. We cannot reflect God's image if sin is in us. And this verse says we're all guilty.

> If you know you've sinned, pause to
> confess your sin to Him—aloud, right now.

B Believe that Jesus is the Son of God and that His death on the cross paid for all your sins. You may be familiar with John 3:16. That beloved Bible verse reads, "For God so loved the world, that he gave his only Son, that whoever believes in him should not perish but have eternal life." What kind of love is that? That God would sacrifice His only Son so we can live with Him! He so wants you to be a Christian, because He loves you.

> If you believe Jesus is God's Son,
> pause to say that to Him out loud.

C Confess your faith in Jesus out loud and to others. Romans 10:9-10 says, "If you confess with your mouth that Jesus is Lord and believe in your heart that God raised him from the dead, you will be saved." Salvation requires your mouth! You must tell both God and others that Jesus is the Lord of your life.

> If you want Jesus to be the Lord of your life,
> begin by asking Him to do that. Ask aloud, right now.
> Then go tell someone! You've become our brother
> in Jesus today. Welcome to the family!

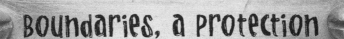

Boundaries, a Protection

No test or temptation that comes your way is beyond the course of what others have had to face. All you need to remember is that God will never let you down; he'll never let you be pushed past your limit; he'll always be there to help you come through it.
1 CORINTHIANS 10:13 MSG

PARK IT!

My good friend Bob, Dannah's husband, is someone who enjoys a good prank (like me). We've had to establish boundaries to our pranking because things can get out of hand pretty quickly. Our pranking rules are pretty simple. The prank cannot cause damage to anyone's stuff. It has to be easy to clean up. And it needs to be enjoyable for the prankee.

Recently for April Fool's Day (a holiday we take seriously), a couple of guys from the high school where I work helped me steal Bob's car. We then removed the school's front doors and carefully parked Bob's car in the lobby. We then posted pictures to Facebook with the comment that if anyone saw Bob, could they please let him know that he was illegally parked.

Bob's car barely squeezed through the doors to our school lobby. What a great prank!

51

About an hour later Bob showed up at school and offered cash rewards to students for the four most successful pranks against me in the next week. He also announced that the rules of pranking had been suspended. The students' eyes lit up like it was Christmas.

Later that day I reminded Bob that I had an attic full of styrofoam peanuts—millions of them!—that I'd collected over the years (there are two things Bob fears: snakes and styrofoam peanuts). I told him I would unleash a styrofoam fury against him, should the pranking get out of hand. The rules of pranking were quickly reinstated.

millions of styrofoam peanuts at the ready

That week my truck was saran-wrapped, it was covered in 1,192 sticky-notes, and my home was listed for sale on Craigslist. But the pranking never got out of control. The students stayed within the boundaries and good fun was had by all (including me).

God wants us to have fun. He doesn't want us walking around bored or unhappy. He created us to enjoy His creation, to enjoy Himself, and to enjoy life. God knows, however, that if we take good things too far, it can be hurtful to ourselves or others. So, like Bob and me, He has set boundaries for us to protect us from that pain.

What do you like to do for fun? **Make a list of some of your favorite freetime activities below:**

_____   _____

_____   _____

_____   _____

_____   _____

_____   _____

What's the most fun you've ever had? **Draw a picture of it in the box provided.**

In this chapter we're going to look at three specific areas where God wants you—as a boy becoming a man—to have boundaries: Girls, gaming, and goofing off. At this stage of your life, with hormones raging, life can begin to seem mixed up and backwards, so let's mix it up a little and tackle this list from back to front.

GOOFING OFF: Sometimes it's fun to go back and study the definitions of words in the Bible in their original languages of Greek and Hebrew. So what does the Bible have to say about goofing off? It never uses those exact words, but it does drill deeply into the issue in a more basic way. It gives us good ground rules on how we should treat others. Remember, though God wants us to be happy and have fun, He also wants us to keep it within boundaries that prevent us from hurting others (or ourselves!).

Happiness is good medicine, but sorrow is a disease (Proverbs 17:22 ERV).

Happiness is good medicine. I love making people laugh. Sometimes though, I've made people laugh at the expense of others, and that's a boundary issue. Paul tells us in Ephesians that everything we say (and do!) should benefit those around us or bring them joy in some way.

Do not let any unwholesome talk come out of your mouths, but only what is helpful for building others up according to their needs, that it may benefit those who listen (Ephesians 4:29 NIV).

In 1 Corinthians Paul reminds us that our bodies are not our own:

Or didn't you realize that your body is a sacred place, the place of the Holy Spirit? Don't you see that you can't live however you please, squandering what God paid such a high price for? The physical part of you is not some piece of property belonging to the spiritual part of you. God owns the whole works. So let people see God in and through your body (1 Corinthians 6:19-20 MSG).

So while the Bible doesn't mention goofing off exactly, we can see there are many scriptures that remind us we're responsible for everything we say and do. We need to make sure our goofing off is always done in a manner that makes others feel good and encourages them in some way. Our words should never be hurtful to anyone, and we need to always obey those in authority over us, like our parents, teachers, and pastors, all the while treating others like we would want to be treated.

GAMING: One of the best things about having kids is getting
to play with their toys and having an excuse to buy the toys I
always wanted but never had growing up. I was a "deprived" child
growing up in a home that never owned a video gaming system. I
can specifically remember the time my family visited a friend's house
and they had a video gaming console connected to their TV. (Brief
pause for mind-blowing memory moment.) Wow. I remember it
like it was yesterday. The dimly lit living room. My parents' voices
in the next room. And this extremely high tech gaming console
my friend Jeremy was calling an "Atari." (This was long before the
high-powered Atari 2600 was unleashed). I could have spent hours
sitting there playing Tank Battle. (Actually I did.) What a game
changer (pun intended!).

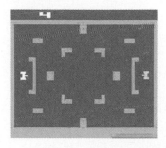

Okay, so gaming has come a long
way since the dawn of Atari, but the
desire to spend hours upon hours
sitting in front of a screen has not. So
what's the problem with it anyway?
Video games don't hurt anyone. Or do
they? Actually they do. Anything—good
things or bad (not just video games)—
when done to excess can be harmful to us.

Listen to this discussion in the Bible:

**"I am allowed to do anything," you say. My answer to
this is that not all things are good. Even if it is true that
"I am allowed to do anything," I will not let anything
control me like a slave (1 Corinthians 6:12 ERV).**

Men need a mission. We long for a sense of purpose—
something to fight for. We want to save the world. Unfortunately,
too many men find a false sense of purpose in gaming. They

become immersed in imaginary battles on the screen and spend so much time playing games like *Call of Duty* that they never develop a real call of duty. In fact, 25 percent of boys will actually become addicted to that false sense of purpose and find it very difficult to control the amount of time they spend gaming.

It's been over thirty years since I was introduced to video gaming, and I still love to play them. I spend many a winter evening playing the latest version of *Madden* with my son on his Xbox One (and if I am honest, I still struggle with wanting to spend more time than I should playing it!) I came to realize though that my time is a gift from God and I need to use it wisely and not waste it all by spending excessive amounts of it doing something that's simply unimportant and potentially destructive.

GIRLS: Up until this point in your life, you were pretty sure that all girls had cooties or some other weird condition, and that if you were to be touched by one of these strange creatures, your skin just might begin melting away. But then one morning you woke up, you went to school, and suddenly, seemingly overnight, girls looked

BOUNCE YOUR EYES

different. Somehow they became majestic beings who began to call to you. Something about them caused you to feel funny on the inside. You find yourself doing anything and everything to attract their attention. (If this hasn't happened to you yet, it will…soon. Just wait!)

As awkward as these feeling can be, they're completely normal. God created this attraction. It started with Adam and Eve, and it continues with us today.

God says, "It is not good for the man to be alone. I will make a helper who is just right for him" (Genesis 2:18 NLT). Girls were God's idea. (And as you become a man, they're starting to seem like a very good idea!)

God has, however, set up boundaries for us when it comes to girls. Let's take a look at them.

GUARD YOUR EYES. As your body changes while you're becoming a man, the bodies of girls around you are changing too. As you're comparing armpit hair with your friends, girls your age are shaving their armpits and beginning to grow into their womanly figures. This can suddenly be very, very appealing to your eyes. You may find yourself wanting to study their feminine frames more than studying for that test you have tomorrow.

The first boundary you need to establish is with your eyes. Listen to these words from Jesus.

Your eye is a lamp that provides light for your body. When your eye is good, your whole body is filled with light. But when your eye is bad, your whole body is filled with darkness (Matthew 6:22-23 NLT).

You must decide now to refrain from lingering looks. You can do this by what we call "bouncing your eyes." When you see a girl your eyes want to linger on, you need to immediately bounce them away from that image, just like bouncing a ping-pong ball off the sidewalk. Your eyes are a gateway to your thoughts, and training your eyes to bounce will make our next boundary—around your thoughts—much easier to keep.

 *guard! guard! guard! guard!*

GUARD YOUR THOUGHTS. Probably some of the biggest battles you'll ever face won't happen on a battlefield or in a sports arena; they'll take place in your mind. Our thoughts consume us. They define us. They have power to control us if we let them, so we must learn quickly to take control of them before they take control of us. We need to set firm boundaries in our thought life.

When it comes to girls, we must make sure to keep our thought life pure. We must not look at girls as objects for our enjoyment, but as what they really are, daughters of our Heavenly Father. The boundaries we set in how we think and act toward girls will be so much easier to maintain if we've trained our brains to think pure thoughts.

So what *should* we be thinking? Well let's take a look at something Paul tells the Philippians.

Fix your thoughts on what is true, and honorable, and right, and pure, and lovely, and admirable. Think about things that are excellent and worthy of praise (Philippians 4:8 NLT).

Paul tells us to direct our attention unwaveringly toward things that are true, honorable, pure, and admirable. The thoughts you have toward your sisters in Christ should fall into one of those categories.

Let me sum it up like this. Suppose you're thinking about a girl. If you wouldn't be willing to tell her father *exactly* what you're thinking about her, you shouldn't be having those thoughts!

GUARD YOUR HEART. One of the most encouraging
scriptures for me is Acts 13:22, where God calls David "a man after his own heart." You see, David wasn't perfect by any means. He messed up big time! And yet, in the end God refers to David as someone who has a good heart like God's. Protecting our hearts needs to be a top priority for us.

David's son Solomon wrote this in Proverbs:

 Guard your heart above all else, for it determines the course of your life (Proverbs 4:23 NLT).

When it comes to girls, we need to be extremely careful to keep our hearts pure. Having a pure heart means we should be looking at (and thinking about) girls in a way that pleases God.

The word "heart" appears almost a thousand times in the Bible, making it one of the most common words in Scripture. Our hearts are obviously important to God because He talks so much about them.

By the way, when the Bible mentions our *heart*, it isn't talking about the physical organ that pumps our blood but rather our thoughts, our motives, and our moral character (who we are when no one else is looking). The thoughts we give our minds to will wrap around our hearts, and out of our hearts those thoughts become actions.

Let's take a look next at those actions.

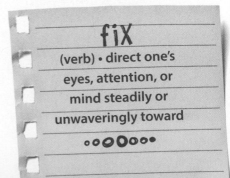
fix
(verb) • direct one's eyes, attention, or mind steadily or unwaveringly toward

GUARD YOUR ACTIONS. If you've successfully set and maintained boundaries for your eyes, your thoughts, and your heart, it will make this final area of *your actions* much easier.

Until you're ready to get married, you should see all girls as your sisters. Period.

Paul writes this to his young friend Timothy:

"Treat younger women with all purity as you would your own sisters" (1 Timothy 5:2 NLT).

What?! That means that you should treat all girls around your age as you would treat your very own sister (*if* you treat your sister nicely, that is; if you don't, you'd better start treating her better, because she's a daughter of the King of kings!).

Just yesterday I had a conversation about this with my niece Molly. Molly is an extremely cute and outgoing sixteen-year-old who's going into her junior year of high school. She gets lots of attention from boys in her school, and she was asking me what her boundaries with boys should be. My answer was that she should treat them all as brothers. I told Molly she shouldn't do anything with boys that she wouldn't do with her brothers. Molly has three older brothers, so she knew exactly what I was talking about. I also told her that the boys at her school should be treating her as a sister—and that if they aren't, she should get away from them!

Molly's three older brothers strongly desire to protect her (sometimes so much so that it annoys her!). They want to defend her from guys who won't treat her the way she should be treated as a daughter of God. Your actions, like those of Molly's brothers, should be for the protection and defense of your sisters in Christ, treating them as if they were your own little sister. **Period.**

Meditation 4

FREEDOM!

W e've spent a lot of time in this chapter talking about boundaries—lines we're not to cross and things we're not allowed to do. It could begin to seem like becoming a godly man is all about the things you can't do. Nothing could be further from the truth. The truth is that you have a loving Savior who made the ultimate sacrifice, in your place, so that you could live a life of freedom. Why did Jesus do this? Because He knew that the results of sin were holding us to a life of bondage. He came to set us free!

Paul writes the following in his letter to the Galatians:

 It is for freedom that Christ has set us free. Stand firm, then, and do not let yourselves be burdened again by a yoke of slavery (Galatians 5:1 NIV).

Wow! That's great news! We're free men! God does give us boundaries, but they're in our life to protect us.

The heavy pads and helmets football players wear hinder their natural movement. They make it harder to run or to throw and catch a football. However, those pads protect the player from injuries that would happen if the pads weren't worn. Injured players can't play. The pads keep them in the game—free to play.

In the same way, God's boundaries keep us in the game of life, ready to perform to our full potential. God has an amazing plan for your life. The boundaries He puts up are actually to free us to live a life uninhibited by the pain sin causes. Those boundaries enable us to see, do, and experience things beyond our greatest imaginations.

You are a free man. Protect that freedom at all costs.

Puzzle Craze

Staying within the boundaries that God has set up to protect our purity is, quite honestly, a battle. It's a fight that we need to fight each and every day. Paul says, *"I have fought the good fight, I have finished the race, and I have remained faithful"* (2 Timothy 4:7 NLT).

Protecting your heart while avoiding the distractions of this world can feel as tricky as traversing an ancient labyrinth that is full of savage beasts. **See if you can avoid distractions and detours as you navigate your way through the following labyrinth on your way to guarding your heart and protecting its purity.**

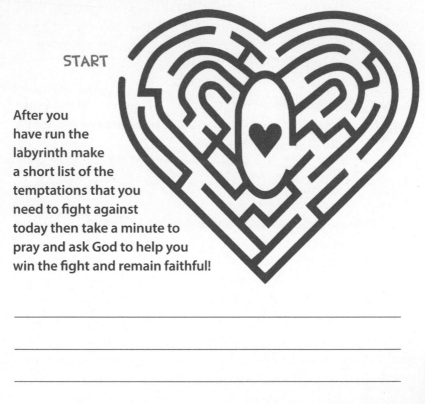

START

After you have run the labyrinth make a short list of the temptations that you need to fight against today then take a minute to pray and ask God to help you win the fight and remain faithful!

_____

_____

_____

_____

Answers to puzzles on page 123.

DIG IN by Studying James 1:12-15

We live in a world full of temptation. We've only briefly touched on a few of the major ones for boys your age. Temptation comes in all shapes, sizes, and forms. Maybe you haven't goofed off a day in your life, you don't own a videogame, and you haven't ever seen a girl (don't laugh, it's possible!). Or maybe those things just hardly ever tempt you. But temptation *will* come in some manner, and when it does, you need to be ready.

Being tempted isn't a sin. Everyone is tempted. Even Jesus was tempted. In fact, the Bible says Jesus was tempted in every way, just so He could relate to us, and we to Him.

It's what we do when temptation comes knocking that defines our character. Jesus' half-brother, James, explains it this way:

12 Great blessings belong to those who are tempted and remain faithful! After they have proved their faith, God will give them the reward of eternal life. God promised this to all people who love him. **13** Whenever you feel tempted to do something bad, you should not say, "God is tempting me." Evil cannot tempt God, and God himself does not tempt anyone. **14** You are tempted by the evil things you want. Your own desire leads you away and traps you. **15** Your desire grows inside you until it results in sin. Then the sin grows bigger and bigger and finally ends in death (James 1:12-15 ERV).

James clearly instructs us to "remain faithful" when we're tempted. He says that God doesn't leave us alone in our struggles, but will always help us with whatever challenges we're facing.

I recently visited one of my former students, Jeffrey, at the US Air Force Academy in Colorado Springs. Jeffrey gave me a personal three-hour tour of the Academy's inner workings. It was absolutely fascinating. One of the more interesting things I learned is that all first-year cadets are given a handbook called *Contrails* that contains important information from American military history, transcripts of important national documents, and details on aircraft, satellites, and munitions in the current air force inventory. Basically it's everything a cadet needs to know, and therefore they have to memorize the whole thing word for word (all 208 pages!).

remain faithful when tempted

We need to be just as prepared as these cadets for the challenging temptations we'll face, so let's break down that passage we read from James 1. **Fill in these blanks:**

1. When you are tempted, you must remain_____.

2. After they have proved their faith, God will give them the reward of _____.

3. God promised this to all people who _____.

4. Whenever you feel tempted to do something bad, you should not say, "_____."

5. _____ cannot tempt God.

6. God himself does not _____.

7. You are tempted by the _____.

8. Your own desire leads you away and _____.

9. Your desire grows inside you until it _____.

10. Then the sin grows bigger and bigger and finally

_____.

Answers on page 124.

Temptation will come—that's a given. The good news is that God is always there to help you overcome it. You need to trust that He loves you and that the boundaries He's put in place are for your benefit. You also need to be prepared. Like the Air Force Academy cadets, you need to make sure you have the right information for any circumstance you find yourself in. That comes from digging into God's Word on a regular basis so you're familiar with His battle handbook.

LOOK Inside yourself

I've been asked hundreds of times: "Is it a sin to _____?" (You fill in the blank.) Everyone wants to know where that line is—cross over it, and your action becomes sin. How much screen time is too much? When do I have to obey my parents? What about girls? Paul writes to Timothy instructing him to "flee youthful passions" (2 Timothy 2:22). What does it mean to *flee* something?

If we're creeping up on the line that separates good from evil, trying to get as close as we can—would that be considered *fleeing*? I don't think so. To flee means turning and running as far and as fast as we can from anything God does not want us to do.

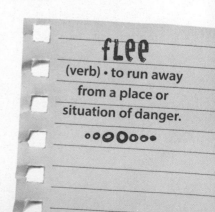

flee

(verb) • to run away from a place or situation of danger.

The bottom line goes back to these words of Jesus: "Do to others whatever you would like them to do to you" (Matthew 7:12 NLT).

Ask yourself: "Am I treating others the way that I want to be treated? How do I know if I'm doing that?"

Well, you need to treat people like God would treat them. The Bible says that *God is love*. **Listen to how the Bible describes love:**

4 Love is patient, love is kind. It does not envy, it does not boast, it is not proud. **5** It does not dishonor others, it is not self-seeking, it is not easily angered, it keeps no record of wrongs.

6 Love does not delight in evil but rejoices with the truth.

7 It always protects, always trusts, always hopes, always perseveres.

8 Love never fails (1 Corinthians 13:4-8 NIV).

A great way to compare your life to God's definition of *love* is to go back to that passage and insert your name everywhere the word "love" is used or referred to. **Let's try it. Fill your name in the blanks below:**

_____ **is patient.**

_____ **is kind.**

_____ **does not envy.**

_____ does not boast.

_____ is not proud.

_____ does not dishonor others.

_____ is not self-seeking.

_____ is not easily angered.

_____ keeps no record of wrongs.

_____ does not delight in evil but rejoices with the truth.

_____ always protects, always trusts, always hopes, always perseveres.

_____ never fails.

How did you do? Are the statements above true about you?

We need to be striving every day to help make sure they are. The easiest way to not cross over the boundaries God has put in place is to run from them. *Flee* them! Then run toward loving God and loving other people.

FLEE THEM!

REACH UP and TALK to GOD

Jesus, I need Your help. I want to live my life in a way that glorifies You in everything I do. I realize I need to have better boundaries when it comes to _____

_____

and _____. I would like to ask Your forgiveness for _____

_____.

Jesus, please help me to have pure thoughts and motives. Help me guard my eyes and my heart from things that distract me. Help me see others the way You see them. And remind me to run from things that might cause me to sin, and instead to run toward You!

Eat This, Do That

And God said, "Behold, I have given you every plant yielding seed that is on the face of all the earth, and every tree with seed in its fruit. You shall have them for food."

GENESIS 1:29

I have a problem for you to solve in this chapter. Pay close attention because we're going to ask you to make a decision for an 11-year-old. His story's made up — but it might sound like yours or a friend's.

Meet Jeff. He's always been the heaviest guy in his class. Last year he ran the mile for gym class, and ended up barfing before he could finish. That was a wake-up moment. He began paying more attention to how he fared when doing other activities his friends did. He began noticing that he didn't have as much energy as his friends did when they hung out together.

Just this year Jeff started to enter puberty and noticed big changes in his body. One of the biggest was that he gained even more weight! He shared all this with his dad, who took him to the

FOOD!

doctor to make sure nothing was wrong with him that was causing the low energy. The doctor said the problem could possibly be the combination of inactivity—a by-product of his addiction to online gaming—and a constant diet of potato chips, cheese fries, and hot baked chocolate chip cookies.

Jeff decided to try out for basketball, but he knew it would mean eating differently, turning his computer off, and getting active. He did just that.

Now he loves feeling healthy, and he's able to run long distances without feeling like he might toss his lunch. And guess what? Jeff made the basketball team, and has had a great year.

Here's the problem: this weekend Jeff has been invited to a basketball team backyard campout. The invitation says there's going to be games, and food, food, FOOD!

Jeff is nervous. What if it's all pizza and donuts and candy? What if they have cheese fries—because who can say no to those?

Food and exercise are hot topics in our world today. I think they're important too. Is that because I think you have to be buff to be popular?

No, that's as shallow as it gets.

God says our value is determined way more by what's on the inside than what's on the outside.

But we also need to remember that we're to glorify God with our bodies, and that our bodies are God's temple. If our purpose is to glorify God and He's living in our bodies, then we'd better take seriously the care and keeping of our bodies. This goes way beyond being thin. It's about being physically fit.

[Physical fitness is wise.]

It simply isn't wise to risk your health by being overweight or by filling yourself with junk food. If your body's purpose is to glorify God, you want your body strong for the tasks He calls you to do. Besides, God specifically instructs us to glorify Him when we eat and drink (1 Corinthians 10:31). Wisdom says, "Take care of the body God has given you for this amazing ride we call life."

Be wise. Pursue fitness. That does *not* mean you'll necessarily be thin. Some of us are naturally thin and some of us have naturally thicker, stronger bodies. But you'll know when you're *fit*. You can feel it in the strength of your being.

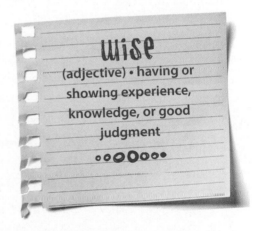

wise
(adjective) • having or showing experience, knowledge, or good judgment
∘∘◉ ◯∘∘•

Let's see if our meditation today will help us become wise about being fit. You can become an expert consultant for Jeff. You'll get to advise him later in the chapter. What are we waiting for? The campout he's invited to is happening soon, so we've got to tell him what to do about it!

Meditation 5

Food, Your Fuel

I 'm not here to dictate what you should or should not eat, but to help you discover food's purpose and how to achieve it. From there, I'll trust you to use your own judgment—each time you eat.

One big reason for this is that everyone's body is different. Some things that seem perfectly healthy to one person can make another person not feel well. Wheat, for example, makes my friend, Bob, less mentally clear and more sluggish. He's not allergic to it, but he feels a whole lot better when he fuels himself with a lot of protein like nuts, meat, and dairy. When Bob creates his MyPlate it includes a lot more meats and a whole lot less in the grains section. Bob has decided, however, that his favorite French dip—a sandwich with lots of bread that you dip in delicious meat gravy—is okay *once in a while*. With food, you should avoid being legalistic and just use wise judgment based on what works for your body. But the point is: you *should* be judging what you eat.

Okay, with that settled: let's dig in.

DIG IN by Studying Genesis 9:1-5

Today we're diving in to the Bible at the very end of the story of Noah and the ark. My coauthor Dannah and her husband, Bob, could have filled in nicely for Noah and his wife in that they love animals. They have twenty to be exact, including Moose, the 85-pound labradoodle who thinks he's a lap dog (whom I mentioned previously). They also have two horses, two fainting goats, two cats, seven llamas, one miniature donkey, three peacocks, and two chickens.

But let's talk about animals before Noah's flood. You see, the animals were apparently rather tame before the flood, which may explain why Noah and his wife had no problem getting them into the ark. But after the flood, everything changed.

judge what you are eating

Use a brown marker to circle all the different types of critters mentioned in the passage below. *(Hint: There are four.)*

1 God blessed Noah and his sons and said to them, "Be fruitful and multiply and fill the earth. **2** The fear of you and the dread of you shall be upon every beast of the earth and upon every bird of the heavens, upon everything that creeps on the ground and all the fish of the sea. Into your hand they are delivered. **3** Every moving thing that lives shall be food for you. And as I gave you the green plants, I give you everything. **4** But you shall not eat flesh with its life, that is, its blood. **5** And for your lifeblood I will require a reckoning: from every beast I will require it and from man. From his fellow man I will require a reckoning for the life of man.

Use a black or gray marker to draw a square around the two words that describe how these critters are going to feel about humans after the flood.

I guess if I were a big old juicy salmon or a nice fat beef cow, I'd have "fear" and "dread" of you if you were going to eat me too! Isn't it interesting that humans didn't always eat meat? Did you know that? For thousands of years, humans had been instructed by God to limit themselves to eating green plants.

Use a green marker to draw a heart around the thing that humans ate before the flood.

Before the flood, humans were primarily vegetarians. Our bodies today are classified as omnivores (able to digest both meat and vegetables), but God's original instructions to humans were to eat veggies. We must need them! Carnivores—those created to eat meat, such as wolves—have short intestinal tracts, so meat can go through them quickly without getting stuck there and rotting. Vegetarians—those created to eat vegetation, such as cows—have longer intestinal tracts, so food goes through them slowly. **What do you think humans have? Write it below.**

_____

That's right! God created us with longer intestinal tracts. In the very beginning, God instructed Adam and Eve what they should eat based on how He constructed our bodies: "And God said, 'Behold, I have given you every plant yielding seed that is on the face of all the earth, and every tree with seed in its fruit. You shall have them for food'" (Genesis 1:29).

FOOD IS FUEL

You gain wisdom about your body in two ways. First, you experience the consequences of how well you care for it—both good and bad. Second, wisdom comes from knowledge, which is the focus of our next two chapters. From these things you're able to use good judgment. Just as a car requires gasoline to run, our bodies require fuel. That fuel is food. But we think of food as entertainment; not fuel. Cinnamon rolls. Butterfinger Blizzards. French fries. Pizza. These are staples in many of our diets. But they won't give us energy. If you want energy you need carrots, whole wheat toast,

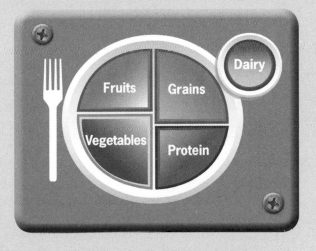

bananas, blueberries, and spinach. (I know. I like them as much as you do, but I'm determined to take care of God's temple by eating well.) The US government has designed this simple MyPlate graphic so you can see what each meal should look like.

There's a copy of this with a Bible verse and eating plan on the last page of this chapter so you can cut it out and put it somewhere to monitor how well you are using food as fuel.

Why did God change His directions after the flood? Some Bible scholars think that there was not enough vegetation to eat, so God made this allowance to eat meat. The fact is, avoiding meat isn't right or wrong.

It's just wise to be balanced in our approach. God makes lots of allowances for us when it comes to food, but we were designed to eat the stuff He grows: vegetables, fruits, and whole grains. Those should be the bulk of our diet.

Let's be honest: most guys don't like that stuff. In fact, I'd love to share my world-famous wings recipe with you (but you've got to eat some greens with them!)

Over time, we've adapted to needing and getting our protein from animal products such as eggs, meats, and dairy products. So, these should now also be an important part of our diet.

What shouldn't be in our diet in excess? Hmm...maybe we should talk about that too.

LOOK Inside yourself

Everyone has certain foods and drinks they really like. What are some of your favorites? Use one of the boxes on the next page to draw the logo of your favorite fast-food restaurant. (No, I'm not getting paid to advertise for anyone. I just want to make a point.) And use one of the boxes on the next page to draw your favorite junk food.

Now, write: "It's okay!" inside each box. Unless you have a medical condition that requires you not to eat that stuff, it's an acceptable allowance. But remember: it's wise to be fit.

Here are a few things (not just food) that *aren't* wise for the human body. **Circle any that you may be guilty of.**

- getting a sunburn
- going on a diet that causes rapid weight loss
- withholding food entirely
- over-exercising
- eating *only* junk food
- bingeing on candy

- bingeing on soda
- eating no fruits, vegetables, or whole grains
- using drugs
- getting drunk
- smoking

A wise man doesn't do any of these things to his body and tries to break any bad habits that have crept in. He also takes care not to be too extreme about anything. Not too much junk food. And not being overly strict (legalistic) about healthy food.

One of my favorite Bible verses says, "Whoever fears God will avoid all extremes" (Ecclesiastes 7:18 NIV).

Now it's time to put on your expert consultant hat and help Jeff. **Based on everything you've just learned, what would you tell Jeff to do this weekend?**

A "Just relax, Jeff. Eat what you want and what you like, but only when you are feeling hungry."

B "Either pack a bunch of veggies in your bag or plan on starving. You don't want to go back to that lifestyle!"

C "Eat up, guy! You never know when you'll have the perfect excuse to eat all the junk food you want again. Besides, one night never hurt anyone."

What did you pick based on everything you've learned in this lesson? For the record, I would advise Jeff to go with choice A. The problem with choice B and with choice C is exactly the same. If Jeff allows food to control him to the point he's fearful of eating anything but a carrot (choice B), or goes crazy with junk food (choice C), he's letting food control him.

We don't want to be controlled by anything but God's Holy Spirit. On the other hand, we also want to be sure we aren't careless or lazy. When Jeff was struggling with his weight, he could have said, "God loves me just the way I am, and that's good enough for me." Did God love him just the way he was? You bet! Did God have better plans for him? You know He did! Jeff should be pretty excited about the fact that he worked hard and was rewarded by feeling better and making a good basketball team.

NOT TOO MUCH JUNK FOOD!

Puzzle Craze

The things named in this puzzle should be eaten more than anything else, but your diet doesn't have to be restricted to them. (Remember, God makes allowances.)

ACROSS

6. World's biggest fruits
7. A princess once slept on one of these

DOWN

1. They help with vision
2. Red veggies that are really fruits
3. Chinese staple that's white
4. A Veggie Tale Madame
5. These are good baked and loaded

Answers to puzzles on page 124.

Now, let's make a few of those foods more fun by matching them up to some partners that could create some really yummy after-school or bedtime snacks. **Using three of the things you've just found in the crossword puzzle, fill in the blanks below:**

peanut butter and _____

_____ and ranch dip

_____ and whipped cream

Since this is all about judgment, there's really no right or wrong answers for what you wrote above. (If you like peanut butter with spinach, who am I to judge?)

HOW ABOUT SPINACH YOGURT? JUST A LITTLE TASTE? AWW, COME ON!

REACH UP and TALK to GOD

Hi, Jesus! I knew / didn't know **(circle one)** that You originally created human beings to eat vegetables, fruits, and grains. It's good to know You make allowances, like when You let Noah eat meat. Here are a few things I'd like to eat as allowances: _____, _____, _____, _____. And here are a few things You created me to eat that I like a lot: _____, _____, _____, _____. Thanks for making these for me. Help me to never be too extreme in how I eat, but I do want to be fit for Your glory. Give me self-control when I need it and wisdom to approach what I eat with good judgment.

Sincerely,

_____

(sign here)

FUEL YOURSELF FOR HIS GLORY

*So whether you eat or drink or whatsoever you do, **do it all for the glory of God*** (1 Corinthians 10:31).

Keep track of how well you fuel yourself for one week. Think of a way to reward yourself at the end of the week, if you've eaten "for the glory of God."

TOTALS

GRAINS

VEGETABLES

PROTEINS

FRUITS

DAIRY

exercise, your strength

I discipline my body and keep it under control.
1 CORINTHIANS 9:27

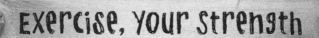

When I was in eleventh grade, my dad brought home this high tech contraption he called a mountain bike. I'd ridden bicycles all my life, but never anything like this. This bike had eighteen speeds, and when I started pedaling, I felt I could climb Mount Everest on it.

Thus my bicycle trekking career was born.

That summer Dad and I conquered the trail that follows the C&O Canal: 184.5 miles from Cumberland, Maryland to our nation's capital, Washington, DC. What an adventure it was, but we were only getting started.

The following summer, we pedaled out of our driveway in Addison, Pennsylvania and made our way through Maryland and West Virginia to

Front Royal, Virginia, then pedaled 109 winding miles in the Blue Ridge Mountains to the southern end of Virginia's Skyline Drive. On the final evening of our trip, as we were sitting at a picnic table in Loft Mountain Campground, my dad uttered four words that would change my life: "We could keep going."

get started in the direction God is leading

"What do you mean?" I asked.

"We could keep going," he said, "like all the way across the country."

Something clicked in me when my dad spoke those words. I realized he was right. The only thing between me and riding my bicycle all the way across the country was about 900,000 pedal strokes!

FLESH VS. SPIRIT = TWO SUMO WRESTLERS

But it had to wait for the next summer, when we boarded an Amtrak train headed for Seattle, Washington. Once there, we simply started pedaling toward home.

When we set out from Seattle, I truly didn't realize the magnitude of our journey. If I had, I probably would never have attempted it. I wouldn't have had the faith to complete such an adventure. At that point, however, I didn't need faith to *finish* it, but only the faith to get started.

And that's what I did. One pedal stroke at a time, we pushed homeward. Forty-nine days and 3,184 miles later we arrived in our driveway in Addison, Pennsylvania. It was the adventure of a lifetime. It still amazes me that I was able (or crazy enough) to do it.

Sometimes God will call us to do things we think are impossible—things we're sure we'll never be able to do. But just as with my bicycle trip, we just need the faith to believe that if we'll get started in the direction God is leading, He'll help us do what's impossible on our own.

It's really a battle between your *flesh* and your *spirit* (which houses God's Spirit). Our flesh and spirit are like two sumo wrestlers. The one you nurture the most will always be stronger and win. Feeding your spirit and calling your flesh into servitude and submission in little things assures that you'll win in the big things.

We feed our flesh (our body) by sleeping in late, overeating, watching TV shows that aren't good for us, procrastinating when we have homework, and being too lazy to brush our teeth.

We feed our spirit when we get up early to read our Bibles, eat veggies when we want donuts, turn the TV off when it gets nasty, do our homework before we hang out, and take good care of our teeth.

These are simple examples, but you get the idea. Feeding our flesh fuels selfishness. Feeding our spirit fuels self-control. That's why the Bible says, "Walk in the Spirit and you shall not fulfill the lust of the flesh" (Galatians 5:16 NKJV). Another translation (NLT) puts it this way: "Let the Holy Spirit guide your lives. Then you won't be doing what your sinful nature craves."

Our flesh doesn't naturally desire to do things that glorify God, but will easily work to dishonor Him. That's why we struggle so much with sin and temptation. Left to our own devices we sleep in instead of getting up to read our Bible, watch TV shows that train our mind to laugh at sin rather than to honor God by thinking of things that are pure, or indulge in too much junk food rather than having the conviction of self-control. The list goes on and on. Instead of glorifying God with our bodies, we do a great deal to deny Him.

What I want you to hear is this:

[**Your spirit has a job to do: to glorify God.**
So your body better get its attitude straight! **]**

Meditation 6

Exercise, Your Strength

We all want instant gratification. We want the easy way out. Every time I see a new product or invention that promises a super-easy way to get physically fit, lose weight, or get rich, I know it's not reliable. Just like those vibrating belt machines that were so popular in the 1950s. All you had to do was loop the belt around you and let the machine shake you into the muscle man you've always wanted to be.

The truth is that increasing the strength of your body, mind, and spirit isn't easy, but it is important. God requires us to have discipline in all we do, and even after thousands of years of inventions and medical breakthroughs, there still is no other way to stay healthy and fit than to eat well and exercise often. I wish it was different, because I'd love to just strap on that belt. But it would only shake my belly and make me hungry.

Now, let's dig in and see if we can get some wisdom from the Bible on what God thinks of fitness.

DIG IN by Studying
1 Corinthians 9:24-27

One of the coolest guys in the Bible is the apostle Paul. Not only did God use him to say some of the most challenging things ever written, but Paul loved something we do: *sports*. In the letters he wrote, Paul made it clear that he was a big sports fan. His letters mention wrestling, boxing, running, throwing...all the big sports of his day. Paul compared our training as those who love Jesus to the training of an athlete. **Using a marker the color of your favorite sports team, circle every instance in the verses below that refers to any sport.**

24 Do you not know that in a race all the runners run,

but only one receives the prize? So run that you may obtain it.

25 Every athlete exercises self-control in all things. They do it to

receive a perishable wreath, but we an imperishable. **26** So I do not

run aimlessly; I do not box as one beating the air. **27** But I discipline

my body and keep it under control lest after preaching to others I

myself should be disqualified (1 Corinthians 9:24-27).

Paul isn't saying that running is spiritual nor is he saying that boxing is the secret to a happy Christian life. These are word pictures that help us understand how we should be living our spiritual lives—like athletes who work hard because there's a prize to be won. We should be training hard to win the prize of pleasing God.

Look at verse 25 and circle the word that every athlete exercises. (Hint: It's not legs, or abs, or lungs, but something you can't see.) Use the word you find to fill in the blank.

[
The main reason we should exercise our bodies

is to practice _____ - _____ _____.
]

Overeating and lack of exercise are both self-control problems. Self-control is a fruit of the Holy Spirit (it should be present in every Christian). Your life, and mine, should be full of self-control.

I look at exercise differently from the way a lot of other people do. I don't think it's primarily about getting physically fit, as wise as that is. Exercise is primarily about developing self-control so that your spirit—not your body—controls your decisions.

Puzzle Craze

Grab your markers and draw two very different pictures in the boxes below. Let one illustrate what a life without self-control looks like; let the other illustrate a life with self-control. Use the Bible verses in each box to help you draw these pictures.

NO SELF-CONTROL Proverbs 5:23

SELF-CONTROL 1 Corinthians 9:25

He will die for lack of self-control; he will be lost because of his great foolishness (Proverbs 5:23 NLT).

Every athlete exercises self-control in all things. They do it to receive a perishable wreath, but we an imperishable (1 Corinthians 9:25).

A life of no self-control is ugly and full of stress and destruction. But a life of self-control provides for peace and reward. Which one are you choosing?

LOOK Inside yourself

Meet Greedy Gavin, Gluttonous Garrett, and Lazy Luke. These are the characters that take over your body when self-control isn't exercised. Let's figure out if any of them are taking up space inside of you.

GREEDY GAVIN: "I'm Gavin and I can't get enough 'stuff,' whether it's skateboards, money, friends, attention, or food. I love it all. Sometimes greedy people are called 'fat cats,' but I don't like that nickname. I'm not fat. What does fat have to do with it? I just like to have as much of everything as I can have. I figure that in the end, life is measured by how much we end up owning."

Is Greedy Gavin inside you? If so, consider these words of Jesus:

"Watch out! Be on your guard against all kinds of greed; life does not consist in an abundance of possessions" (Luke 12:15 NIV).

self-con·trol

(noun) • control over your feelings or actions; controlling yourself

Write Gavin a quick note. Use Luke 12:15, and be as kind but as firm as possible. Gavin needs a new outlook! Where does he have mistaken ideas? Where might his "stinking thinking" lead him in the future?

_____

_____

_____

_____

GLUTTONOUS GARRETT: "Hey there! I see what you said to Gavin, but I'm not nearly as bad as he is. I'm Garrett, and generally speaking, I just like food. Admit it—food is good. I'm always afraid if I don't eat it now I won't be able to get it later, so I make sure I get all I want. The beautiful thing is, I'm not a fat cat either! I can eat and eat and eat…all I want. It's what I live for."

Do you recognize Garrett? If so, read the Bible verse below.

As I have often told you before and now tell you again even with tears, many live as enemies of the cross of Christ. Their destiny is destruction, their god is their stomach, and their glory is in their shame. Their mind is set on earthly things (Philippians 3:18-19 NIV).

Write Garrett a note using Philippians 3:19. Maybe it would be good for him to see that gluttony isn't about size, but about attitudes of the heart. Is food for nourishing healthy bodies? Or is food supposed to be our source of thrills? Maybe you can help Garrett find a couple of things more important in life than yummy food.

_____

_____

_____

_____

LAZY LUKE: "Hey there! I'm Luke—Lazy Luke—and I'm proud of it too. Why not take it easy? I have all I need. I live in a nice house with a housekeeper (my mom) who cooks all my meals and makes my bed. I pretty much watch TV whenever I'm not forced to be in school. I don't do much homework because I'm smart enough to get A's on my tests. Life's boring, but it's easy. Gotta go—time for some gaming."

Does this sound familiar? It's time to apply the Bible verses below to your life.

A little sleep, a little slumber, a little folding of the hands to rest—and poverty will come on you like a thief and scarcity like an armed man (Proverbs 6:10-11).

Diligent hands will rule, but laziness ends in forced labor (Proverbs 12:24).

Write a note to Luke. Those verses should give you plenty of background information. Maybe you can help him see what his future looks like if he refuses to get off of that couch!

Newton's first law of motion states that an object in motion tends to remain in motion, and an object at rest tends to remain at rest. What's that say about you?

_____

_____

_____

_____

Reach UP and Talk to GOD

JESUS, this chapter was a tough one to take! Just between You and me, I can be honest though. I know You know me inside and out, so why not? I do / do not (**circle one**) struggle with weight. I do / do not (**circle one**) make an effort to exercise. I do / do not (**circle one**) pay attention to what I eat. I am / am not (**circle one**) exercising self-control. I know it matters. I know the world is watching; I know that if You live in me and I have a relationship with You, I'll look more and more like You all the time, and that includes self-control. I don't want to love my appetites and my stomach (or my couch and my TV shows) more than I love You. I also don't want to make big promises I can't keep, so help me start small. For the next 21 days, I want to do these two things so I can grow in self-control over food and exercise: I'm going to _____ and _____. And I'm going to tell my mom / dad / another adult (**circle one**) about it so they can keep asking me how it's going!

I've got this! With You, that is.
All my love,

_____
(sign here)

The Challenge: Spirit Versus Body

Exercise works best in pairs. Ask your dad or a guy you respect a lot to exercise with you for 21 days. Try reading the Bible before you do, so you can remember it's really about your spirit and self-control, not your body.

Sign this Spirit Versus Body Challenge with your dad. Post it on your fridge or the bathroom mirror so you can see it each morning when you're getting ready for the day.

> I discipline my body and keep it under control
> (1 Corinthians 9:27).

Every day for the next 21 days, we, _____

and_____, will together pray quietly and read the

Bible, and then exercise for _____ minutes. If one of us misses a

day, that person will _____ for the other.

Signed: _____*Date:*_____

Signed: _____*Date:*_____

Here are some things you can do for each other if you miss a day: clean out the other person's closet, or complete some chore (when it's the other person's turn for it) such as mowing the grass, walking the dog, or taking out trash.

THE CHALLENGE: SPIRIT VERSUS BODY

I discipline my body and keep it under control
(1 Corinthians 9:27).

Keep track of the discipline of your body for the next 21 days. Under each day of the week, enter the miles you walked or ran. Any exercise you do for 15 minutes counts as one mile. If it's a slow activity such as golf, it counts as walking. A fast activity like basketball counts as running.

	WEEK 1	WEEK 2	WEEK 3
MONDAY			
TUESDAY			
WEDNESDAY			
THURSDAY			
FRIDAY			
SATURDAY			
SUNDAY			

your Body, a Source of Life

*Then God blessed them and said, "Be fruitful and multiply.
Fill the earth and govern it. Reign over the fish in the sea, the birds
in the sky, and all the animals that scurry along the ground."*

Genesis 1:28

Face it, it's pretty uncomfortable, even in a book, to talk about the parts "under our zipper." Even when we're talking guy-to-guy, it seems weird.

But that shouldn't be.

We know that we're fearfully and wonderfully made and that God created our body to allow us to glorify God and enjoy Him forever. Satan, as our mortal enemy, does his best to take this awesome gift and introduce shame and awkwardness to the conversation. *Reject that.* Don't be afraid to talk about hard things with your mom and dad.

So, here it is. This chapter is about the uniqueness of our uniquely male organs and the physical changes that occur…*down there.*

It all begins with puberty. In the simplest terms, puberty is the physical process that transforms a boy's body into a man and a girl's body into a woman. Puberty affects our bodies in many different ways.

Why are girls often taller than boys when they're your

age? Because puberty causes you to grow taller, and most girls reach puberty first, usually between ages 8 and 13. Guys' bodies can start to transform as early as 9, but most boys start to feel their bodies change between 10 and 14. So girls get taller first, but they usually don't end up taller once guys catch up. In fact, the average American man is five inches taller than the average American woman.

Puberty is amazing, but so many things are happening at once that you might feel like your body is out of control! You're physically changing from boy to man, and although we've mentioned some of these things before, it doesn't hurt to review them. Here's what to expect.

1 **Your hair will grow, but not just on your head.** Some guys will grow more hair than others, but there's no doubt that you'll start seeing it under your armpits, on your arms and legs, in your pubic area (the area around your penis), and possibly on your chest. Eventually, you'll also grow hair on your face, and before you know it, you'll be ready to shave.

2 **You'll get zits and pimples.** One of the worst things about puberty is that your glands grow and you start to sweat more. As a result, your skin and hair will become more oily and create a great environment for acne. The word "acne" comes from an old Greek word that means "skin eruptions." Obviously, pimples have been around for a long time! The good news is that there are things you can do to reduce acne, like gently washing your face at least twice a day and being reasonable about what you eat.

3 **Your voice will change.** Inside your throat, at the top of your trachea (or windpipe) is your larynx. It's also called your "voice box." Your vocal chords stretch across it. During puberty, your larynx grows and your vocal cords grow longer and thicker, causing your voice to sound lower. It doesn't happen overnight, so there are times when you'll sound a little funny. Don't worry. It won't take long to get your manly voice up and running.

4 **You'll grow everywhere.** Your hands and feet and brain will grow; so will your muscles; so will your penis and testicles. Your internal organs will grow too. In fact, back to the larynx—the cartilage protecting it will grow during this time, giving you something few girls have—an Adam's apple.

what is an Adam's apple?

Your growth spurt will last at least two to three years. At its peak you may gain four inches in height in a single year.

5 **You'll stink more.** Remember those growing glands that produce more oil and sweat? Normally our bodies produce more than a liter of sweat per day, but most of this evaporates before we even notice it. The more you sweat, however, the more your body will give off an odor that makes you unpleasant to be around.

Our body sweats in order to keep from overheating, but we can also sweat when we're in stressful situations or experience strong emotions. Sweat also plays a role in fighting infections. *Why* you sweat doesn't matter; what matters is how you deal with it. You'll need to use deodorant each morning and shower every day if possible, particularly after intense physical activity.

Your body will also start producing a chemical called testosterone. Testosterone is the hormone that builds stronger bones and muscle. It's what builds the body of a man. Men produce seven to eight times more testosterone than women. (Women have their own version of testosterone, called estrogen; it does for the female body what testosterone does for the male body.)

Testosterone helps develop your sexual organs and opens up a whole new world just for guys. One of the most incredible (and sometimes confusing) things that will happen to you is that there'll be many more times when your penis will harden and become "erect" (thus it's called an "erection"). This may happen at awkward moments and be beyond your control. (If this happens when you're in close proximity to other people, you may have to get creative in slipping away.) It will even happen occasionally while you sleep.

Now that your body's producing testosterone, your testes will also produce sperm. The word "sperm" is from a Greek word that means "seed," and it is truly the seed of life.

Sperm from a man is what fertilizes the egg of a woman during sex and enables a woman to have a baby.

The whole process is amazing!

awkward word heading your way!

Since sperm continues to be produced down there, it needs a place to go. And there's only one place for it to go: out the urethra, the same tube that urine (pee) comes out of. Muscles at the base of your penis will contract about every second, and this forces (or ejaculates) the semen out of the penis in up to five spurts. This is called ejaculation.

Ejaculation almost always occurs during an erection (though, of course, not every time you have an erection). It can happen while you're sleeping, which is called a nocturnal emission, although almost everyone calls it a "wet dream." This is totally natural, but still surprising. It's no fun waking up with wet sheets, but it's nothing to be ashamed of, nor is it anything you can control. Hey, that which doesn't kill us makes us stronger, and this is one of those things. Ask your dad or another respected adult male in your life how to handle it before it happens, and it will feel a lot less awkward. (Then get those sheets into a laundry basket quickly!)

AWKWARD WORD ALERT!

Prepare yourself. I'm going to say it (err...well, I'm going to write it). It's the M-word. Brace yourself...Masturbation. There, it's out. Now, let's deal with it. It's a word that nobody likes to talk about but that almost every young man (and old man) will struggle with at some point in his life. Just reading about it probably makes you feel awkward and squirrely (just writing about it is somewhat uncomfortable for me!), but it's something we must talk about because if we don't you will most likely be left feeling all alone in your battle against sin. That is exactly what the enemy wants you to feel—alone, dirty, worthless, and shamed, but that's not what you are. I'm here to tell you that you are not alone.

The Bible doesn't have a lot to say about masturbation. In fact, it doesn't directly mention it at all. But the Bible does address the feelings that come along with it—specifically, lust. Jesus said, that "everyone who looks at a woman with lustful intent has already committed adultery with her in his heart" (Matthew 5:28). Lust is a *strong longing* for something that is not ours. In this instance, we're talking about girls that we aren't married to. When we engage in thoughts about girls that lead us to satisfy our own sexual desires, it becomes sin.

So what do you do? Those feelings will come. They will. And not always because you want them to, but sometimes just because you are a guy. Period.

It's not the initial thoughts that are sin though. It's when they linger. It's when you continue to think them and act out on them that it becomes sin. Sin separates us from God, and

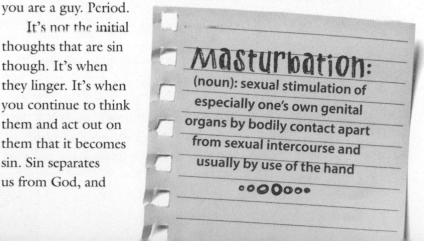

Masturbation:
(noun): sexual stimulation of especially one's own genital organs by bodily contact apart from sexual intercourse and usually by use of the hand

that's when the feelings of guilt and shame come in and cause us to feel pretty miserable about ourselves. The best solution is to have someone in your life that you can talk to about it. Someone you can trust and check in with. Someone who will ask you about it and how you are doing in overcoming it. Your dad would be ideal, but I realize that isn't always possible, so it may be a youth pastor, a mentor, or another male family member. The bottom line is that you are not alone in this struggle for sexual purity, and you need to have someone who can fight for your purity with you.

Meditation 7

Your Body, a Source of Life

All the changes we're discussing are part of God's plan to make men and women distinct and unique and to clearly define our roles. These changes also distinguish boys from men.

Besides being different physically, men are to *act* differently than boys do. Paul speaks about this transition:

When I was a child, I spoke and thought and reasoned as a child. But when I grew up, I put away childish things (1 Corinthians 13:11 NLT).

Here are a few other verses about the things godly men do.

Jesus grew in wisdom and in stature and in favor with God and all the people (Luke 2:52 NLT).

Fathers, do not provoke your children to anger by the way you treat them. Rather, bring them up with the discipline and instruction that comes from the Lord (Ephesians 6:4 NLT).

Husbands, love your wives and never treat them harshly (Colossians 3:19 NLT).

 All Scripture is breathed out by God and profitable for teaching, for reproof, for correction, and for training in righteousness, that the man of God may be competent, equipped for every good work (2 Timothy 3:16-17).

 He has told you, O man, what is good; and what does the Lord require of you but to do justice, and to love kindness, and to walk humbly with your God? (Micah 6:8).

 Have I not commanded you? Be strong and courageous. Do not be frightened, and do not be dismayed, for the Lord your God is with you wherever you go" (Joshua 1:9).

According to these verses, what are some things men are to do?

_____

_____

_____

_____

_____

_____

_____

_____

_____

I want to be very clear on this point. Many people in the world are confused about the differences between a man and a woman. Sexuality may be controversial in our culture, but in most cases that's because our culture rejects God.

God's Word tells us . . .

A time is coming when people will no longer listen to sound and wholesome teaching. They will follow their own desires and will look for teachers who will tell them whatever their itching ears want to hear (2 Timothy 4:3 NLT).

Oh, how the world will squawk and complain when I say this! But that's okay.

Not all men have hair on their chest, or a low voice, or big muscles. Men are different. They may like sports or sewing, football or flowers, country music or opera. They may like blue or pink or red or orange. But one thing is sure: Our physical attributes were designed by God to clearly identify us as male or female.

DIG IN by Studying Judges 13:3-5; 14:5-6; 16:4-21

Superheroes (and supervillains for that matter) are the kinds of guys you'd guess would have a lot of extra testosterone. There are plenty myths and legends about superheroes throughout history. Superheroes usually have at least these four things in common.

1. special strengths

2. special weaknesses

3. at least one archenemy

4. a special purpose

For example, one of my favorite superheroes in Greek mythology is Achilles. After his birth, his mother, Thetis, dipped her infant son's body into the waters of the River Styx, which was believed to offer powers of invulnerability and thus immortality. But as she dipped him, she held him by his heel, so that his heel was untouched by the magical water.

Achilles had special armor made for him. This armor, as well as the immortality he believed he possessed, enabled him to be an amazing hero, the bravest warrior of the Greek army in the Trojan War. In his greatest battle he defeated his archenemy, Hector, leader of the Trojans. Achilles was ultimately killed when he was shot in his unprotected heel with a poisonous arrow shot by Hector's brother, Paris—but not before having fulfilled his special purpose of ensuring the Greek victory over the Trojans.

To this day, the term "Achilles' heel" refers to a profound weakness experienced by a person who has great strengths, a weakness which ultimately can lead to downfall.

Who is your favorite movie superhero?

_____

What special skills does he have?

_____

What is his Achilles' heel, his greatest weakness?

_____

What is his special purpose?

_____

When I think of a man in history who must have had a lot of testosterone, I think of one of the great heroes of the Bible— **Samson**. Here's his story.

During the time God was punishing the Israelites by allowing them to be oppressed by the Philistines for forty years, an angel appeared to Samson's mother and told her she would give birth to a boy—but not just any boy. Her son would be the superhero Samson!

Read this passage and see if you can find the marks of a superhero.

3 "Even though you have been unable to have children, you will soon become pregnant and give birth to a son. 4 So be careful; you must not drink wine or any other alcoholic drink nor eat any forbidden food. 5 You will become pregnant and give birth to a son, and his hair must never be cut. For he will be dedicated to God as a Nazirite from birth. He will begin to rescue Israel from the Philistines" (Judges 13:3-5 NLT). 5 As Samson and his parents were going down to Timnah, a young lion suddenly attacked Samson near the vineyards of Timnah. 6 At that moment the Spirit of the LORD came powerfully upon him, and he ripped the lion's jaws apart with his bare hands. He did it as easily as if it were a young goat. But he didn't tell his father or mother about it (Judges 14:5-6 NLT). 7 Some time later Samson fell in love with a woman named Delilah, who lived in the valley of Sorek.

5 The rulers of the Philistines went to her and said, "Entice Samson to tell you what makes him so strong and how he can be overpowered and tied up securely. Then each of us will give you 1,100 pieces of silver." **6** So Delilah said to Samson, "Please tell me what makes you so strong and what it would take to tie you up securely." **7** Samson replied, "If I were tied up with seven new bowstrings that have not yet been dried, I would become as weak as anyone else." **8** So the Philistine rulers brought Delilah seven new bowstrings, and she tied Samson up with them. **9** She had hidden some men in one of the inner rooms of her house, and she cried out, "Samson! The Philistines have come to capture you!" But Samson snapped the bowstrings as a piece of string snaps when it is burned by a fire. So the secret of his strength was not discovered. **10** Afterward Delilah said to him, "You've been making fun of me and telling me lies! Now please tell me how you can be tied up securely." **11** Samson replied, "If I were tied up with brand-new ropes that had never been used, I would become as weak as anyone else." **12** So Delilah took new ropes and tied him up with them. The men were hiding in the inner room as before, and again Delilah cried out, "Samson! The Philistines have come to capture you!" But again Samson snapped the ropes from his arms as if they were thread. **13** Then Delilah said, "You've been making fun of me and telling me lies! Now tell me how you can be tied up securely." Samson replied, "If you were to weave the seven braids of my hair into the fabric on your loom and tighten it with the loom shuttle, I would become as weak as anyone else." So while he slept, Delilah wove the seven braids of his hair into the fabric. **14** Then she tightened it with the loom shuttle. Again she cried out, "Samson! The Philistines have come to capture you!" But Samson woke up, pulled back the loom shuttle, and yanked his hair away from the loom and the fabric.

15 Then Delilah pouted, "How can you tell me, 'I love you,' when you don't share your secrets with me? You've made fun of me three times now, and you still haven't told me what makes you so strong!" **16** She tormented him with her nagging day after day until he was sick to death of it. **17** Finally, Samson shared his secret with her. "My hair has never been cut," he confessed, "for I was dedicated to God as a Nazirite from birth. If my head were shaved, my strength would leave me, and I would become as weak as anyone else." **18** Delilah realized he had finally told her the truth, so she sent for the Philistine rulers. "Come back one more time," she said, "for he has finally told me his secret." So the Philistine rulers returned with the money in their hands. **19** Delilah lulled Samson to sleep with his head in her lap, and then she called in a man to shave off the seven locks of his hair. In this way she began to bring him down, and his strength left him. **20** Then she cried out, "Samson! The Philistines have come to capture you!" When he woke up, he thought, "I will do as before and shake myself free." But he didn't realize the LORD had left him. **21** So the Philistines captured him and gouged out his eyes. They took him to Gaza, where he was bound with bronze chains and forced to grind grain in the prison (Judges 16:4-21).

Let's take a quick break and come back to the ending of Samson's story later. In the meantime, let's answer Samson's superhero questions.

What special skills did Samson have?

_____

What was his Achilles' heel, his greatest weakness?

_____

Can you name a second weakness of Samson? (Think hard.)

_____

What was Samson's special purpose?

_____

Samson's amazing strength was his special skill. His Achilles' heel was that he would lose his strength if he ever broke the Nazirite vow and had his hair cut. As for the second weakness— Samson could not resist the temptation of a beautiful woman.

As for his special purpose, it's way back in Judges 13:5. His special purpose was to "begin to rescue Israel from the Philistines."

I'm going to add a third weakness to Samson's list and the one that really did him in: *pride*.

Samson's pride got him in trouble his whole life. He forgot that his true strength came from obeying God and following His commands. Every time we let pride slip into our life, we're headed for a fall. As the Bible says, "Pride goes before destruction, and haughtiness before a fall" (Proverbs 16:18 NLT).

When we deviate from God's plan, we're bound to fail. As men, we often try to be independent and accomplish things on our own. This is not only foolish, but also unnecessary. "The LORD says, 'I will guide you along the best pathway for your life. I will advise you and watch over you'" (Psalm 32:8 NLT)

And we know God's pathway for our lives through prayer and through reading His Word: "Your word is a lamp to guide my feet and a light for my path" (Psalm 119:105 NLT).

The good thing is, you're already doing it. You've been studying God's Word throughout this book and praying too. Keep on the path!

Before long, Samson's hair began to grow back. Returning in Judges 16 to his story, we read...

23 The Philistine rulers held a great festival, offering sacrifices and praising their god, Dagon. They said, "Our god has given us victory over our enemy Samson!" **24** When the people saw him, they praised their god, saying, "Our god has delivered our enemy to us! The one who killed so many of us is now in our power!" **25** Half drunk by now,

the people demanded, "Bring out Samson so he can amuse us!" So

he was brought from the prison to amuse them, and they had him

stand between the pillars supporting the roof. **26** Samson said to the

young servant who was leading him by the hand, "Place my hands

against the pillars that hold up the temple. I want to rest against

them." **27** Now the temple was completely filled with people.

All the Philistine rulers were there, and there were about 3,000 men

and women on the roof who were watching as Samson amused

them. **28** Then Samson prayed to the LORD, "Sovereign Lord,

remember me again. O God, please strengthen me just one more

time. With one blow let me pay back the Philistines for the loss of my

two eyes." **29** Then Samson put his hands on the two center pillars

that held up the temple. Pushing against them with both hands,

30 he prayed, "Let me die with the Philistines." And the temple

crashed down on the Philistine rulers and all the people. So he killed

more people when he died than he had during his entire lifetime.

The moral of Samson's story is about humility:
"Pride goes before destruction, and a haughty spirit before a fall"
(Proverbs 16:18).

REACH UP and TALK to GOD

First, fill in the blanks to personalize your prayer and then pray your prayer out loud.

Dear _____
(your favorite name for God),

I recognize that like Samson, I sometimes struggle with pride. Please forgive me. I read in Your Word that this pride leads to a fall. I don't want to fall, so help me to be humble and let others into my struggles. I see another thing in Samson's story that is a struggle for me, and that is _____.
I need help with this. I recognize that I can't win against this temptation alone. Please help me to talk to _____ (an older, wiser, godly man you trust) about this struggle so I don't feel so alone. I realize this step will take a lot of humility, but it will help me overcome my pride. Give me strength to do this, Lord?

In Jesus' name,

_____
(sign here)

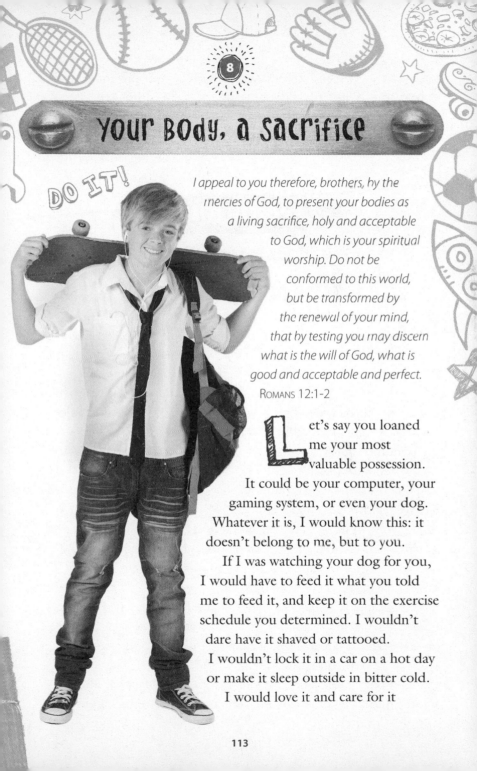

Your Body, a Sacrifice

8

DO IT!

I appeal to you therefore, brothers, by the mercies of God, to present your bodies as a living sacrifice, holy and acceptable to God, which is your spiritual worship. Do not be conformed to this world, but be transformed by the renewal of your mind, that by testing you may discern what is the will of God, what is good and acceptable and perfect.
ROMANS 12:1-2

L et's say you loaned me your most valuable possession. It could be your computer, your gaming system, or even your dog. Whatever it is, I would know this: it doesn't belong to me, but to you.

If I was watching your dog for you, I would have to feed it what you told me to feed it, and keep it on the exercise schedule you determined. I wouldn't dare have it shaved or tattooed. I wouldn't lock it in a car on a hot day or make it sleep outside in bitter cold. I would love it and care for it because it's *yours*, and when you returned for your precious pup, you'd want to find it just the way you left it—healthy, well cared for, and loved the way you would love it.

Guess what? God has entrusted *you* with one of *His* most valuable possessions—your body. How well are you caring for it?

Meditation 8

Your Body, a Living Sacrifice

Have you ever heard of the 10,000 hour rule? Author Malcolm Gladwell has a theory that it takes 10,000 hours of practicing deliberately and correctly to become world-class in any field. Consider the following story written about Eldrick Tont Woods. You may know him better by his nickname, Tiger.

When Tiger Woods was an infant, his dad, Earl, moved his high chair into the garage. This was where Earl practiced his golf swing, hitting balls into a soccer net after work. Tiger was captivated by the swift movement. For hours on end, he would watch his father smack hundreds of balls.

When Tiger was nine months old, Earl sawed off the top of an old golf club. Tiger could barely walk—and he had yet to utter a single word—but he quickly began teeing off on the Astroturf next to his father. When Tiger was 18 months old, Earl started taking him to the driving range. By the age of three, Tiger was playing nine hole courses, and shooting a 48.

That same year, he began identifying the swing flaws of players on the PGA tour. ("Look Daddy," Tiger would say, "that man has a reverse pivot!") He finally beat his father—by a single stroke, with a score of 71—when he was eleven.

At fifteen, he became the youngest player to ever win the United States Junior Amateur championship. At eighteen, he became the youngest player to ever win the United States Amateur championship, a title he kept for the next three years. In 1997, when he was only 21, Tiger won the Masters at Augusta by the largest margin in a major championship in the 20th century. Two months later he became the number one golfer in the world.

So if 10,000 hours of good practice is the formula to be an all-star NFL or NBA player, or one of the world's best chefs or artists or guitar players—why doesn't everyone do it?

I can answer that with one word: *sacrifice*.

Many people might think it would be awesome to golf or play guitar for 10,000 hours, but most don't have the discipline and focus to practice anything for that long. Even harder is having to sacrifice (give up) all the other fun or interesting or important things we'd rather be doing.

10,000 HOURS TO BE AN ALL STAR!

Being the best at something often brings personal glory to the athlete or artist or business tycoon, but over the past few chapters, we've already learned that our goal in life is to bring glory to God, not to ourselves. The cool thing is that the only way we achieve true joy is by obedience to God and a willingness to sacrifice our own selfish desires for His glory.

That doesn't mean you can't still be the world's best golfer. It just means that even if you're not, you'll still be a world-changer.

DIG IN by Studying 1 Corinthians 6:19-20 and Romans 12:1-2

If you've learned anything about your body during our time together, I hope you learned the importance of using your body to glorify God. We've come full circle, and it's time to look once again at the Bible verse we began with. **Grab your green marker (because it is the color of American money) and underline the words "high price."**

19 Don't you realize that your body

is the temple of the Holy Spirit, who lives in you

and was given to you by God? **20** You do not

belong to yourself, for God bought you with

a high price. So you must honor God

with your body (1 Corinthians 6:19-20 NLT).

Use your green marker to circle the name of the one who paid the high price.

Why honor God with our body? Because it doesn't belong to us; it belongs to Him. He bought you with a high price—remember, you were a slave to sin. You were separated from God, and the wages for your sin was death. But when Jesus gave His blood on the cross as payment for your sins, He settled the debt you owed to God. He bought you back, and now you belong to Him.

Are you taking good care of God's possession? Are you giving your body back to Him in service and worship?

Read the verse below and circle the word "bodies" with a green marker. Then circle the two words that describe how we're to present our bodies to God.

➡️ **1** I appeal to you therefore, brothers, by the mercies of God, to present your bodies as a living sacrifice, holy and acceptable to God, which is your spiritual worship. **2** Do not be conformed to this world, but be transformed by the renewal of your mind, that by testing you may discern what is the will of God, what is good and acceptable and perfect (Romans 12:1-2).

one of the hardest things you'll ever do

We're to give our bodies back to God as a "living sacrifice." A *sacrifice* is something important to you that you give up to help someone else. To be a living sacrifice means we give up our own will and way—things that are important to most people—to do things God's way while we live on this earth.

Being a living sacrifice is going to be one of the hardest things you'll ever do.

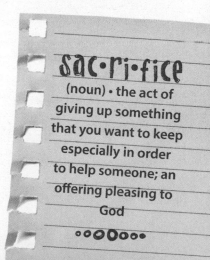

sac·ri·fice
(noun) • the act of giving up something that you want to keep especially in order to help someone; an offering pleasing to God

∘∘◉∘∘•

Puzzle Craze

Unscramble these words.

ILVGIN   ACSFCIERI

_____

_____

We must become living sacrifices. This is hard because we have two choices: we can let our physical desires direct our life, or we can let God's Spirit direct it. (Remember: there's always a battle between our flesh and our spirit.)

Campus Crusade for Christ has developed the following drawings to help us understand this concept of living sacrifice. **Look over these drawings. Under the diagram on the left, write "Unbeliever." Under the center diagram, write "Unsacrificial Christian." Under the diagram on the right, write "Living Sacrifice."**

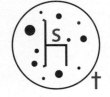   

1._____ 2. _____ 3. _____

Which circle is most orderly? _____

Which two are most out of order? _____ and _____

What do you think the "S" might stand for in these diagrams?

_____

(Hint: it's the root of the word "selfish.")

The circles represents a person's life. Anything inside the circle is a part of their life. In the left circle, is Jesus in the person's life at all? _____

The chair or throne represents the seat of power and authority in a person's life. Who is on that seat in the center circle?

_____

In this center circle, Jesus is in the person's life. Why do you think there isn't more order in this person's life?

_____

_____

When you're on the throne of your life (when you think you're "the boss"), your life is not in order, and you don't live like God's kid. Having *self* on the throne is called "living according to the flesh." But when Jesus is on that throne, you can truly honor God with your body. That's called "living according to the Spirit" or being a "living sacrifice" because everything you do is for Christ.

This is probably a good time to say that Jesus loves you no matter what your circle looks like. He doesn't love people only if they've done a lot for Him, or have their life in perfect order. He loves all people—from inside the womb until they die— no matter what. But we'll find more peace and joy in our lives by being living sacrifices.

LOOK
Inside
yourself

As we continue thinking about being a living sacrifice, let's consider another part of our body: our mouth. Now there's something that can get us into lots of trouble!

There are many proverbs in the Bible that show how a foolish person talks way too much. Has it occurred to you that in many situations, NOT saying something is one way to exercise self-control and be a living sacrifice that glorifies God?

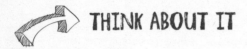 THINK ABOUT IT

How can each of the following be honoring to God?

1. keeping a secret_____

2. not repeating gossip_____

3. counting to ten when angry _____

4. asking someone about their day instead of talking about yours

_____

The ways we can honor God with our speech (or our silence) are nearly endless. When we're children, we speak, act, and reason like a child, just as the Bible says in 1 Corinthians 13:11. Little children have to learn how to control their speech because they tend to be a bit loud, they repeat things they've been told not to, and they don't worry about being unkind. They'll say the most inappropriate things at the most inappropriate times.

A friend of ours had to take her two-year-old son out of church because he'd just learned that church is God's house—and he wouldn't stop shouting during worship, "This is *God's* house! This is *God's* house!" He spoke truth, but not at the right time. And definitely not at the right volume level! You wouldn't do that because you've learned to control your mouth in that situation. But are you guilty in other situations of lacking self control and sacrifice when it comes to your tongue?

If so, confess this right now by writing a list of things you need to work on. (You might use the list above to get ideas.)

1. _____

2. _____

3. _____

4. _____

5. _____

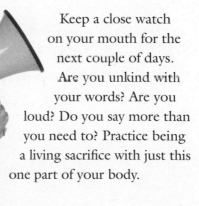

WOW! THIS IS GOD'S HOUSE!

Keep a close watch on your mouth for the next couple of days. Are you unkind with your words? Are you loud? Do you say more than you need to? Practice being a living sacrifice with just this one part of your body.

REACH UP and TALK to GOD

Dear Jesus,

I'm ready to talk about the throne of my life. Am I the boss or are You? Right now, I think I'm living as if the boss is _____ (insert a name—yours or Jesus or maybe even someone else's). I know that unless You are on that throne, things are going to be a mess! Here are some things I've really let You be the boss of: _____ _____ _____. But here are some ways I'm listening to myself instead of listening to You: _____ _____ _____. This world says that I should follow my heart, that I should do what's good for me, that I have to love myself before I can ever love anyone else. But You say I always have to put You and others ahead of me. That's what I want to do. I want to honor You with my body. I want my hands to _____. I want my mouth to _____. I want my feet to _____. And most of all, I want my knees to bow down before You, the One who sits on the throne forever and ever!

Answers to Puzzle Crazes

Answers to puzzle on page 10:
formed, knit, woven

Answers to puzzle on page 11:

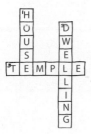

Answers to puzzle on page 22:

Answer to question on page 23:
Circle the word "body."

Answer to question on page 23:
body

Answers to question on page 30:
visible and known

Answers to question on page 32:
1. male, or man, or boy; 2. female, or woman, or girl

Answers to puzzle on page 35:

Answer to puzzle on page 43:
Cleanliness is next to godliness.

Answer to puzzle on page 62:

MORE

Answers to questions on page 64:

1. faithful
2. eternal life
3. love Him
4. God is tempting me
5. Evil
6. tempt anyone
7. evil things you want
8. traps you
9. results in sin
10. ends in death

Answers to puzzle on page 80:

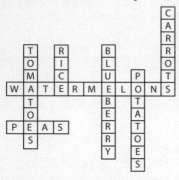

Answer to puzzle on page 118:

living sacrifice

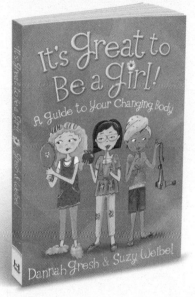

To learn more about Harvest House books
or to read sample chapters, visit our website:

www.HarvestHousePublishers.com

HARVEST HOUSE PUBLISHERS
EUGENE, OREGON